The Chemical-Free Lawn

The Chemical-Free Lawn

The Newest Varieties and Techniques to Grow Lush, Hardy Grass

Warren Schultz

Rodale Press, Emmaus, Pennsylvania

Printed in the United States of America on acid-free ∞, recycled ♺ paper.

Book design by Denise Mirabello
Illustrations by John Carlance
Photographs courtesy of the New York State Turfgrass
Association and Dr. Richard Smiley, Cornell University.

Library of Congress Cataloging-in-Publication Data

Schultz, Warren.
    The chemical-free lawn.

    Bibliography:
    Includes index.
    1. Lawns. 2. Organic gardening. I. Title.
SB433.S365 1989   635.9′647   88-26352
ISBN 0-87857-799-8 hardcover
ISBN 0-87857-801-3 paperback

Distributed in the book trade by St. Martin's Press

2 4 6 8 10 9 7 5 3 1   hardcover
          10 9   paperback

CONTENTS

INTRODUCTION

The good old, clean-cut American lawn is back in style. We love our lawns, especially when they're neat and trim. Lawn care is the most popular gardening activity in the country, outpacing vegetable, flower, fruit, and houseplant gardening. In fact, more people tend lawns than read books, go to movies, or watch sports on TV. There are 5 million acres of home lawns in the United States, with something in the neighborhood of 150 trillion grass plants under cultivation. Americans spend $6 billion a year to keep them looking good.

Why?

The lawn is more than something to fill space between the sidewalk and the front door. Good lawns are worth money. They add value to real estate. A well-maintained yard will increase a home's value by as much as 15 percent. Lawns help to muffle noise, moderate temperature, reduce allergy-causing dust and pollen, control erosion, improve soil, and purify water. Lawns cushion the legs and keep dirt out of the house.

But the value of a home lawn may go deeper than that. Lawns seem to symbolize safety, comfort, and well-being. John Falk, a scientist at the Smithsonian Institution's Chesapeake Bay Center for Environmental Studies, says the love of lawns is in our blood, or at least in our genes.

Falk theorizes that we've built lawns to re-create the surroundings in which the human race was born. "I think human preference for short grass with scattered trees is genetic, and represents our evolutionary history as Sudan organisms," he says. "We spent a good chunk of the formative years of the evolution of the genus *Homo* trying to survive in a savannah." Falk believes that Manhattan's Central Park looks strikingly like the savannahs of Africa, where fossils of early hominids are found. "There exists something called habitat preference. Animals have learned that certain places are good for your health and certain places aren't good for your health. You put a squirrel down in a prairie and it would go crazy, for example."

But that genetic preference doesn't necessarily include manicured grass, clipped to ½ inch and doused with chemicals to eliminate every weed. Falk thinks the modern high-maintenance lawn is an aberration. We may have a habitat preference for short grass, "but short is relative," he explains. "In some cultures short has been defined as 5 or 6 inches. Sometimes in our culture it's an inch and a half." He cites the medi-

eval period, when a "flowery mede" was considered to be an ideal turf. "That was basically a lawn sprinkled with all kinds of short-statured flowering plants. There were little daisies, and scarlet pimpernels, and all kinds of lovely little plants that today might be considered weeds."

Although there is historical record of grassy garden carpets in the Persian Empire, the lawn as we know it is a recent invention. Some say that the lawn was born from the pasturing of animals close to the home in the days when wild animals roamed through Europe. The area around the house, closely cropped by grazing animals, came to be a symbol for safety.

In the medieval era lawns took on a new form. Sod was dug from pastures, planted on estates, and mowed by hand with scythes. But only the rich and titled could afford the labor required to establish and maintain them.

It wasn't until the nineteenth century that the lawn came home, and Edward Budding made the lawn available to everyone with space for it by inventing a tool to maintain it — the lawnmower.

Budding was an engineer at a textile factory. Watching the blades of a textile machine cut fabric one day in 1830, it occurred to him that the same action and type of machinery could be used to cut grass as well. He took the necessary parts home with him and fashioned a rudimentary machine, experimenting with it in his backyard under the cover of night. When his 19-inch-wide machine went on the market, he described mowing as "amusing, useful, and healthful for everyone."

That may have been the last time that anyone used the word "amusing" to describe lawn mowing, and today, tending the typical American lawn is not healthful at all. On the contrary, it can be downright dangerous.

THE LAWN AS A CHEMICAL SPONGE

Homeowners apply an estimated *5 to 10 pounds of pesticide* per acre of lawn each year. Our gardens and lawns receive the heaviest pesticide applications of any land area in the United States, according to a 1980 report of the National Academy of Sciences.

Many people are concerned about the cavalier use of pesticides. "It's awfully tough for the home gardener to develop the degree of care that's necessary to use chemicals safely," says Eliot Roberts, director of the Lawn Institute, a seedmen's association. "It's just asking too much. An awful lot of people are using pesticides, and they don't know what they're doing. The result is damage to their properties and their neighbors' properties, pollution of soils, and contamination of water. It's a very sorry situation."

Millions of homeowners are relying on lawn care services to apply those pesticides. Business has been booming. From the mid-1960s to the mid-1980s, the industry grew at a steady rate of 25 to 30 percent *per year.* But letting someone else douse your lawn with chemicals doesn't ensure safety.

Lawn-care companies maintain that the chemicals they use are safe because they have been registered by the Environmental Protection Agency (EPA). That's a misrepresentation, "a downright fraud," says Jay Feldman, coordinator of the National Coalition Against the Misuse of Pesticides. The EPA grants registration to chemicals that have not been proven hazardous (and even to some recognized as hazardous if their economic benefits outweigh the risks). Feldman points out that this is quite different from being proven *safe*. And the tests cited have been far from complete. Hardly any of the registered lawn care chemicals have been tested thoroughly for their chronic effects on health, including cancer and mutagenicity.

Between 1947 and 1972, tests were made of 35,000 pesticides, including some 600 active ingredients, but only for acute effects. There were no standards for chronic health problems such as cancer, genetic damage, and birth defects. Then, in 1972, Congress ordered the EPA to retest and reregister all of these active ingredients. But as of March 1985, the EPA had retested and reregistered only 16 of them. For the great majority that have not been retested, the possible chronic effects remain unknown.

Of the dozen or so most popular over-the-counter pesticides, nearly all are suspected of causing serious long-term health problems. Many are carcinogenic. Others may cause mutations or sterility.

Many are highly toxic. And all of them can have acute, immediate effects on people who are chemically sensitive.

The chemical 2,4-D is the most commonly used herbicide on home lawns. Lawn service trucks carry tanks full of it. Garden center shelves are lined with bottles and cans of it. But 2,4-D is far from safe. The chemical, formerly a component of the defoliant Agent Orange, contains traces of highly toxic dioxins. Skin exposure to 2,4-D has resulted in acute delayed nervous system damage in humans. Other possible effects include skin rashes and irritation to the eyes, throat, and respiratory tract. Recent evidence against the chemical is even more damning. A study commissioned by the National Cancer Institute linked 2,4-D with increased incidence of lymphatic cancer. In Massachusetts, an advisory committee of the state departments of Environmental Quality Engineering and Public Health stopped just short of urging a ban on the use of 2,4-D. The committee recommended that "2,4-D use should be restricted to areas in which human exposure can be kept to a minimum. Broadcast methods of application that potentially expose the general population should be stopped."

Other common chemicals in lawn service trucks and bottles at the store are just as dangerous.

Dursban (or chlorpyrifos) and diazinon are widely used insecticides. Both are organophosphates, and can affect the central nervous system. Overexposure to chlorpyrifos through skin absorption, inhalation, or ingestion, can result in profuse sweating, nausea, blurred vision, lack of muscle coordination, and tightness in the chest. The chemical has caused chronic health effects in the kidneys, liver, and marrow, and had mutagenic effects in some laboratory tests.

Exposure to diazinon causes eye irritation and skin rashes, and inhibits cholinesterase, a bodily chemical necessary for the proper function of the nervous system. Other symptoms include headaches, dizziness, flulike symptoms, blurred vision, tightness in the chest, and muscle twitches. There is also some evidence that diazinon causes birth defects.

The fungicide benomyl is often the first choice against lawn diseases. But the EPA has classified benomyl as a possible human carcinogen. Tests have shown that it causes birth defects and decreased sperm counts in laboratory animals.

And the list goes on and on. Captan is a carcinogen and mutagen; carbaryl is a fetotoxin and suspected carcinogen; dicofol, which contains DDT, is a dermatoxin; oftanol is a neurotoxin; malathion is a carcinogen and mutagen; mecoprop is a mutagen; methoxychlor causes kidney, liver, and testicular damage; thiram causes nerve damage, and trifluralin is a carcinogen.

Along with the very real toxic effects, an estimated 45,000 chemically sensitive people in the United States suffer such symptoms as nausea and vomiting, swollen eyes, rashes, headaches, body aches, twitching, depression, anxiety, irritability, angry outbursts, sleeplessness, anorexia, chest tightness, and coughing.

Fortunately, the tide has begun to turn against chemical lawn treatment. Legislation that restricts the use of lawn chemicals is on the books in counties and states across the country. And lawn service companies report that business began tailing off in the mid 1980s. At universities and research laboratories, scientists have turned their attention to low-maintenance, low-chemical techniques. Breeders are bringing out new grass varieties that resist both diseases *and* insects. New research confirms that organic fertilizers are better for the lawn, and that cultural practices like mowing and watering can beat weeds. And researchers are learning that common pesticides actually harm the lawn.

Eliminating chemicals doesn't mean settling for a second-rate lawn. But it requires looking at your lawn in a new light.

GRASS GARDENING

The first American turf specialists referred to lawn maintenance as "grass gardening." That gets to the heart of the matter, and takes much of the mystery out of lawn care. If you're a gardener you already know many of the solutions to lawn problems. What do you do when weeds crop up in your flower bed? You don't call a flower care service to take care of them. You hoe or pull the weeds yourself. You can do the same for a lawn. When diseases strike your tomato plants, you shop for resistant varieties. The same goes for grasses.

Think of a grass plant as you would a pepper plant, a geranium, or a perennial like a phlox or poppy. Choose varieties as carefully as you choose a variety of sweet corn. Consider what any plant needs — good soil, sunlight, food, and water — and you're on your way to a healthy lawn.

This book presents a step-by-step program for building and tending a beautiful, low-maintenance, chemical-free lawn. You can, with the help of this book, do it all at once, or you can take it slowly and build a better lawn a little bit at a time. You'll learn how mowing, watering, and fertilizing can solve problems, and you'll learn how to recognize and eliminate weeds, insects, and diseases.

You *can* establish a beautiful, self-service lawn. And whether you're starting from scratch or improving your old lawn, you can do it all without chemicals.

1

WHAT'S WRONG WITH YOUR LAWN?

What's wrong with your lawn? Is it weeds? Disease? Insects? Maybe it's just the wrong grass in the wrong place. How bad is your lawn? Should you dig it up and start all over? Or can it be saved?

Most of us are perfectly capable of fixing our own lawns, but before we can fix them we have to be able to figure out why they're broken. That's a skill very few of us possess. Luckily, it's not hard to learn. And acquiring that diagnostic skill is certainly worthwhile. The lawn is a remarkable system. Identify the problem and you're likely to find the cure to several ills. That's

because a disease, weed, or insect infestation is a sign that the system has broken down.

Diagnosis means looking at your lawn like you've never looked at it before. You have to get to know the grass and the soil beneath it. That involves keeping track of the state of your lawn and noting improvements when you take action.

First, look at the soil. A lawn is only as strong as the soil beneath it. The texture, structure, and fertility of the soil under your lawn will dictate many of your lawn care practices, including watering, fertilizing, and even choosing a type of grass. You can check the structure and fertility of your soil yourself. Or your Cooperative Extension Service or a soil lab can test for pH as well as nutrient content and organic matter.

KNOW YOUR SOIL

Let's start at the beginning. What is soil, and what does it do? Soil is constantly being formed by the same forces that formed it originally: climate and decaying plant matter. It is made up of minerals, organic matter, water, and air. Without sufficient amounts of each, grass just won't grow.

The relationship between soil and plants is a complementary one. Plants decompose to provide organic matter to the soil, and roots aerate the soil and break it down into smaller particles. In turn, the soil provides support and nutrients for plants. The soil must be porous as well as fertile, so that air and water are both readily available to the roots. Two terms are used to define the porosity of the soil — texture and structure.

Soil *texture* is determined by the relative amounts of different-sized particles it contains. Particle size ranges from gravel, the largest, through sand and silt, down to clay, which is microscopic. Although most of us are aware of the problems that clay soils cause, clay can store and pass along nutrients better than silt and sand.

Soil *structure* refers to the groupings of individual particles into larger pieces called granules. Freezing, thawing, wetting, drying, and penetrating plant roots help form granules. The structure of the soil determines its pore space. In good soils, half of the bulk is pore space. This space holds either air or water. In heavy soils, consisting mainly of fine clay particles, the pore space may be too small for plant roots, water, or air to penetrate readily. In sandy soils, on the other hand, the pores will be too large, allowing water and nutrients to drain out rapidly.

Taking texture and structure into account, soils are classified into four basic groups — gravels, sands, loams, and clays.

No one would try to grow a lawn in *gravel*. Under the broad descriptions of *sandy* soils there are gravelly sands, coarse sands, medium sands, fine sands, and loamy sands. *Loamy* soils include coarse sandy loams, medium sandy loams, fine sandy loams, stony silt loams, and clay loams. *Clay* soil mixes with other particles to form stony clays, gravelly clays, sandy clays, silty clays, and clays.

How can you tell which type you have? The easiest way, though not the most accurate, is by hand. Dig up a shovelful of soil from your lawn, pick up just a pinch, and rub it between your fingers. Sand feels gritty. Silt is powdery like talcum powder. Clay is hard when dry, slippery when wet, and rubbery when moist. To get a more accurate picture of your soil's structure, wet a handful and squeeze it into a lump. Now roll the lump between your hands to see if it will form a cylindrical thread. Clay is cohesive and can be molded into a long, thin ribbon that cannot be broken easily. If the soil won't retain any shape, it is largely

TESTING YOUR SOIL TYPE

Judge the relative amounts of sand, loam, and clay in your soil through a simple test. Pour 5 inches of dry soil into a 1-quart canning or mayonnaise jar. Fill the jar with water and fasten the top securely. Shake it thoroughly, then let it settle for 24 hours. The soil types will have settled out into layers, with sand on the bottom, silt in the middle, and clay on the top. Measure the layers for a rough percentage of soil types in your soil. For example, if you have 5 inches of soil in the jar, with 1 inch of clay and 2 inches each of silt and sand, then the soil contains 20 percent clay and 40 percent each of silt and sand. Congratulations! You're working in loam.

1. Clay soil contains about 60 percent clay, 30 percent silt, and 10 percent sand.

2. Clay loam is 35 percent clay, 35 percent silt, and 30 percent sand.

3. Loam is 20 percent clay, 40 percent silt, and 40 percent sand.

4. Silt loam is 15 percent clay, 60 percent silt, and 25 percent sand.

5. Sandy loam is 10 percent clay, 20 percent silt, and 70 percent sand.

6. Loamy sand is 5 percent clay, 10 percent silt, and 85 percent sand.

sand. If the cohesiveness falls somewhere in between, the soil is loamy.

Once you've determined the soil's structure and texture, it's time to assess its acidity and fertility. Home soil and pH test kits are available, but the easiest and least expensive way is to send a soil sample to your state's agricultural (land-grant) college or Cooperative Extension Service. Call the local office and request a soil test bag. It should include complete instructions for gathering a soil sample, but here's an idea of what is involved.

It's best to take a sample when the soil is neither wet nor bone-dry. With a soil sampling probe, trowel, or spade, dig 6 to 8 inches into the soil. Remove a slice of soil about 1 inch thick from the side of the hole. Trim the slice into thirds along its length, discard the two outer thirds, and put the inner third in a bucket or can. Repeat the procedure at five or six other places scattered about your lawn. Mix all of the samples together and dry them indoors overnight. Then send the sample off to the testing service in the container provided.

When the results come back, two to four weeks later, check them against the fertilizer recommendations in Chapter 4. As you'll read there, you don't necessarily want to take the lab's advice as gospel. There are some new ideas about how much fertilizer your lawn really needs, and it's much less than was previously thought. The recommendations will also probably come back in terms of chemical fertilizer: add so many pounds of 10-10-10 or 20-10-5.

Chapter 4 also tells how to convert those figures to the equivalent for organic fertilizer.

While you're waiting for the results, you can take a good look at your grass.

WHAT'S YOUR BRAND OF GRASS?

Do you know the make of your car? Of course. The brand of your electric range? Probably. Chances are you even know the make of your lawnmower, and you keep track of the varieties of tomatoes, lettuce, and beans planted in your vegetable garden.

Now, what kind of grass is your lawn? Sorry, but "green" is not a good enough answer. Here's an easier question: How many types of grass are in your lawn (not counting quack grass and crabgrass)? Just one? Not likely. Most home lawns consist of two or three kinds of grass.

Unless you've recently seeded the whole lawn yourself, you probably haven't the faintest idea what's growing there. And even if you chose and seeded the grass mixture yourself five or ten years ago, the grass that's there now is probably not the same as the grass you put down. Over the years, the proportions can change dramatically as the dominant forms force out the weaker ones.

Do you really need to know your lawn this intimately? Not if you're willing to pay a lawn service hundreds of dollars a year to douse your lawn with chemical fertilizers and hazardous pesticides, herbicides, and fungicides. Not if you're content to allow your lawn to decline every year because of weeds, insects, diseases, or a climate that's unsuited to the grasses growing there. But if you want a good lawn, one that's easy to care for, then you first need to learn the names of those little green plants.

Grasses may look alike to the casual observer, but even those that grow under the same general weather conditions can have very different cultural requirements. One might do best when mowed low, while another is better off mowed an inch higher. One might require a lot of water, another less. The lawn's makeup is especially important when you are diagnosing and treating diseases. Some diseases won't touch certain types of grasses. If you know your lawn is all Kentucky bluegrass and you've learned that powdery mildew rarely strikes this species, then you're that much further ahead when trying to identify a disease. You literally can't mow, fertilize, or water your lawn properly unless you know the names of the grasses in it.

It's not hard to make a reasonable guess at what's in your lawn. If you live in the North, there's a 70 percent chance that at least part of it is made up of Kentucky bluegrass. In the South, it's probably bermudagrass. But you have to know for certain. You can narrow the field considerably by consulting the list of grasses that follow. Then you're going to have to get down on your hands and knees on the lawn, or dig up a clump of your grass and study it carefully.

You can identify a grass type by the characteristics of these parts, their shape, length, colors, and so on. Study the diagram here for identification. Better still, if your grass is actively growing at this time, dig up a few plants and bring them inside for a closer look.

The first distinction made between grasses is whether they are cool-season or warm-season — that is, if they grow best in spring or fall, or if they do most of their growing in the summer. Cool-season grasses are planted in the North; warm-season grasses are the choice for the South. That's an easy way to reduce the possibilities by half, unless you live in the transition zone, where both types are grown.

The following diagnostic blueprints on the following pages are divided into northern and southern grasses.

NORTHERN GRASSES

First look at the leaf *texture*. "It's easy to tell grasses apart by their texture," says Dr. T. L. Watschke of Pennsylvania State University. "That's the first thing you make a

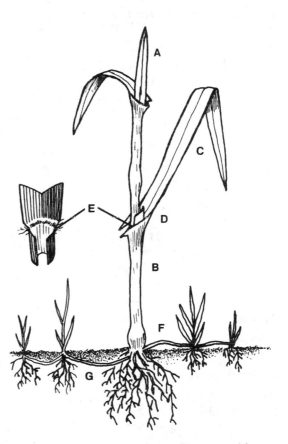

See the box, Parts of a Grass Plant, on this page to identify the parts in this illustration.

PARTS OF A GRASS PLANT

To identify a grass species, you have to be able to recognize the parts of the plant.

A. The *bud leaf* is the emerging new growth at the top of the plant.

B. The *leaf sheath* is the outer wrapping that encloses the stem.

C. The *leaf blade* is the part above the sheath, the blade of grass you mow.

D. The *auricle* is the collar on the outer side of the leaf at the junction of the sheath and the blade. (Not all grasses have auricles.)

E. The *ligule* is a thin sheath or ring of hairs inside the leaf at the collar.

F. The *stolon* is a propagative stem that creeps aboveground, with roots at each node.

G. The *rhizome* is similar to a stolon, but it is a stem that grows underground.

decision about." Texture is the width of the leaf blade. If the leaf is more than 6 mm (about ¼ inch) wide, the grass is classified as coarse-textured. If it's less, it is fine-textured.

If the leaves of your grass are more than 6 mm wide and you live in the North, the grass is almost certainly one of these coarse-textured northern lawn grasses: tall fescue, annual ryegrass, pasture-type perennial ryegrass, orchardgrass, timothy, or quack grass. Of this group, only perennial ryegrass is a desirable turfgrass, and it's by far the most common of the lot. But read on to make sure.

Tall fescue has a sawlike blade margin (leaf edges), a sheath with a reddish base, and a short ligule and auricle. The leaves in the budshoot are rolled rather than folded. If they are folded, you are looking at **orchardgrass.** If the sheath is reddish but the blade margins are smooth, it's *annual ryegrass*. If the sheath is not red, and there are rhizomes, that indicates **quack grass.** If the sheath is not red and you find no rhizomes, you have **timothy.**

If the blades are less than 6 mm, the plant is red-textured. The grass could be Kentucky bluegrass, annual bluegrass, rough bluegrass, fescue, creeping fescue, Chewings fescue, hard fescue, turf type perennial ryegrass, creeping bentgrass, or colonial bentgrass.

Let's check the most obvious first: **Kentucky bluegrass.** This common grass is

WHAT GRASS IS IT? NORTHERN GRASSES

Grass	Texture	Blades	Stolons
Annual bluegrass	Fine	V-shaped	No
Annual ryegrass	Coarse	Smooth-margined	No
Colonial bentgrass	Fine	Veined	No
Creeping bentgrass	Fine	Veined	Yes
Fescues	Fine	Narrow, veined	No
Kentucky bluegrass	Fine	Blunt, V-shaped	No
Perennial ryegrass	Fine	Veined	No
Rough bluegrass	Fine	Blunt, V-shaped	Yes
Tall fescue	Coarse	Shiny below	No

characterized by leaves folded in the bud-shoot. The blades are not veined but have transparent lines on either side of the mid-vein rib. The tip is boat-shaped rather than pointed. The auricle is absent, the ligule is short, the sheath is smooth, and there are rhizomes.

Perennial ryegrass has folded leaves in the budshoot, and auricles are present. The leaves are shiny below, with promi-nent veins on the upper surface. The sheath is smooth and reddish at the base.

Red, Chewings, creeping, and hard fescue have no auricles. The blades are narrow. The margins of the blades are rolled, and veins are prominent.

Rough bluegrass has stolons rather than rhizomes. The leaves are light green, with shiny undersides.

Annual bluegrass has leaves folded in the budshoot, no auricles, V-shaped blades with boat-shaped tips, and no rhizomes. The leaves are shiny, the ligules are long, and seed heads are often showing.

Colonial bentgrass has leaves rolled in the budshoot. Veins are prominent in the leaves. It usually has rhizomes instead of stolons. The ligules are short.

Creeping bentgrass has leaves rolled in the budshoot, prominent veins, and well-developed stolons. The ligules are long. The grass forms a dense canopy.

Use the checklist on pages 6 and 7 to identify the grasses in your lawn.

Rhizomes	Auricle	Ligule	Sheath	Vernation (Budshoots)
No	No	Long	Reddish	Rolled
No	Clawlike	Obtuse	Reddish	Rolled
Yes	No	Short	Split	Rolled
No	No	Long	Split	Rolled
No	No	Obtuse	Smooth, red	Folded
Yes	No	Short	Smooth, flat	Folded
No	Yes	Obtuse	Smooth	Folded
No	No	Short	Light green	Folded
No	Short	Short	Reddish	Rolled

SOUTHERN GRASSES

If you live in the South, your lawn probably consists of one or more of eight common grasses. There are four coarse-textured types—bahiagrass, carpetgrass, centipedegrass, and St. Augustinegrass. The leaves of **bahiagrass** tend to be folded, and it is the only one of the four that will show rhizomes along with stolons. **Centipede-grass** has blunt tips on the blades. The blades of **St. Augustinegrass** are pointed. **Carpetgrass** is similar to St. Augustinegrass, but it has a distinctive light green color.

The fine-textured southern grasses include bermudagrass, blue gramagrass, buffalograss, and zoysia. **Bermudagrass** is the most common grass throughout the South. There are several types, ranging in texture from fine to medium and in color from light to dark green. All types are characterized by their strong, flat creeping stolons, and in some cases by scaly, stout rhizomes.

Blue gramagrass is not nearly as common. Its most notable feature is the grayish-green color of its basal leaves.

Buffalograss is a native prairie grass

WHAT GRASS IS IT? SOUTHERN GRASSES

Grass	Texture	Blades	Stolons
Bermudagrass	Fine to medium	Flat, pointed 1.5-3 mm wide	Yes
Bahiagrass	Coarse	Flat, folded 4-8 mm wide	Yes
Blue Gramagrass	Fine	Flat, toothed 1-2 mm wide	No
Buffalograss	Fine	Curled, grayish-green 1-3 mm wide	Yes
Carpetgrass	Coarse	Pointed 4-8 mm wide	Yes
Centipedegrass	Coarse	Flat, blunt 3-5 mm wide	Yes
St. Augustinegrass	Coarse	Flat, pointed 4-10 mm wide	Yes
Zoysiagrass	Fine	Flat, stiff 2-4 mm wide	Yes

valued for its drought tolerance. The blades are grayish-green and curled.

Zoysia is noted for its slow growth rate and very tough, stiff leaves.

Use the checklist on pages 8 and 9 to identify the grasses in your lawn.

TRANSITION ZONE GRASSES

If you live in the transition zone between North and South (see the map on page 17 of Chapter 2), you may have both cool-season and warm-season grasses in your lawn. But it's not too hard to tell them apart. Their growth habits give them away. Warm-season grasses generally brown out at the fall frost, and green up again only after the weather warms in the spring. Northern grasses may stay green all winter and brown out during the heat of the summer.

TAKING A CLOSER LOOK

Now go back out to your lawn and check to see how much of it matches the grass in your hand. If there are other spe-

Rhizomes	Auricle	Ligule	Sheath	Vernation (Budshoots)
Yes	No	1–3 mm long	Split	Folded, rolled
Yes	No	1 mm long	Overlapping	Folded
No	No	0.1–0.5 mm long	Round	Rolled
No	No	0.5–1 mm long	Round, open	Rolled
No	No	1 mm long	Flat	Folded
No	No	0.5 mm long	Gray, hairy	Folded
No	No	0.3 mm long	Compressed, round	Folded
Yes	No	0.2 mm long	Flat	Rolled

cies present, identify them. Are the species scattered evenly throughout the lawn, or are there discrete patches in the shade, near the sidewalks, and so on?

Jot down the approximate percentage of each grass species in your lawn. If there are definite patches of one type or another, make a map which shows them.

Now that you know what kind of grass you've got, make an honest appraisal of how it looks. Use a checklist to rate the grass all through the growing season, spring, summer, and fall. Mark the dates when it first greens up in the spring, when it begins to turn brown and go dormant in the summer, and when it stops growing in the fall.

Next, measure your lawn. You have to know approximately how many square feet you're tending to judge how much water and fertilizer to apply. If your lawn is an irregular shape, try to break it down into squares or rectangles to make measuring easier. You can pace off the distances or use a 50- or 100-foot hose to measure the lawn. Hoses will even help you measure circles and triangles, provided you haven't forgotten your geometry lessons.

Once you've measured the lawn, assess its general health. Wait until the grass is growing vigorously, perhaps after the second mowing of the season. Give the lawn two or three days to recover from the mowing, then take a walk out to examine it.

Look at the color of the grass. It should be a moderate green. If the overall color is faded, with brown-and-green blades, there could be problems with soil fertility, moisture, or disease. Note that while a deep,

rich, blue-green color may look nice, it may indicate an overfed turf.

Next, check the thickness of the turf. A healthy 4,000-square-foot lawn will have something on the order of 3 million grass plants. It should be thick enough so that you can't see the soil at all. If you can see soil, there is room for weeds and you need to take action.

While you're looking down at the turf, check the thickness of the thatch layer. Thatch is the buildup of matted grass clippings, roots, and stolons that sits on the surface of the soil. Don't be surprised if you see some. In general, thatch is *beneficial* for lawns if it is less than ½ inch thick. A thicker layer may keep out water, air, and fertilizer, while harboring insects and giving rise to diseases. Heavily thatched lawns aren't as hardy as those that are well maintained. They tend to dry out quickly and turn brown at the least hint of drought.

Where does thatch come from? It's not a natural result of leaving clippings on the lawn, as was once thought. The culprit is usually chemicals that halt the natural decomposition of clippings, stems, stolons, and rhizomes. If you remove the thatch and cut out the chemicals it won't come back.

This would be a good time to check the soil for drainage and compaction. Stick a screwdriver into the soil in several places. If you have trouble sinking the blade in to the handle, you've got a compaction problem.

Next, set up a sprinkler and run it for 1 hour. Then wait about 15 minutes and dig a core sample from the soil — a hunk of sod and soil about 3 inches wide and at least 6

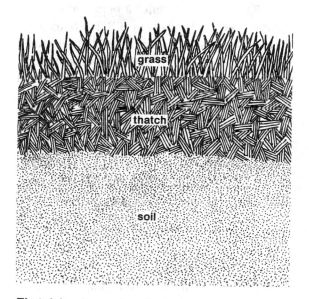

Thatch is a layer of matted grass clippings, roots, and stolons.

inches deep. In well-drained soil, water will have penetrated the full depth of the sample. Look also for a deep, rich color, indicating a high content of organic matter. The grass roots should run completely through the 6-inch soil sample.

WEED WATCH

How about the weeds in your lawn? Unless it's Astroturf, there will be some. A lawn can look good with 10 to 20 percent weeds. A lawn that's up to half weeds can still be renovated. But if the weeds make up more than 50 percent, you need to start from scratch and rebuild the lawn.

Sheila Daar of the Bio-Integral Research Center in Oakland, California, tells how to estimate the number of weeds in your lawn without getting down on your hands and knees and counting each one. Stretch a length of hose, rope, or string diagonally across your lawn. With a notepad and pen in hand, stride along this line and look down at your toe with every step. If there's a grass plant in front of your toe, mark G on the pad. If there's a weed, mark W. After you've marked off every step along the line, pick it up and place it in the other diagonal, to make an X with your previous path. Again, mark a G or W on the pad for every step you take.

When you're finished, count up the Gs and Ws. Suppose you took 100 paces and have 50 Gs and 50 Ws on your pad. Your lawn is 50 percent weeds, and needs help. If you have 80 Gs and 20 Ws, you've got 20 percent weeds in the lawn. That may be a tolerable level. If you think your lawn looks weedy, you can take steps to improve it as outlined in Chapter 7. Continue monitoring as you work on the lawn to see if your methods are having any effect. And keep in mind that the weed population of your lawn will change through the growing season. Some weeds are more prevalent in the spring, others in the summer. You can use the guides in Chapter 7 to identify the weeds as you monitor them.

In addition to calculating the weed percentage, look for especially weedy areas. If you see clumps of weeds in certain spots, that's an indication of an underlying problem. The problem could be from traffic. Well-traveled paths are often weedier than the rest of the lawn. It could be from compacted soil, improper use of herbicides, or either too much or too little moisture (caused by poor drainage or poor soil structure). It could be the aftermath of a grass disease that has allowed the weeds to move in. It could be the result of scalping the lawn while mowing.

How can you tell? Monitor. Clear out the weeds, reseed, and keep a close eye on that spot. Check to see if water sits there, if the mower scalps because of bumps or humps, if the area gets a lot of traffic. Check for a broken water line. If you're still puzzled, take a soil sample to check for compaction. Sure, you want to get rid of the weeds. But first you want to find out why they're growing there so that you can keep them from coming back.

That's the key to a lawn program: evaluate, monitor, remove, and repair. When it comes to weeds, there's no hard-and-fast rule as to how many are too many. Only you can decide how many weeds it takes to ruin a lawn, or even what's a weed and what isn't. It wasn't long ago that clover was commonly included in lawn seed mixes. Today, all kinds of chemicals are employed to eradicate it from suburban lawns. As far as chemical lawn care companies are concerned, the tolerance level for weeds is zero. That attitude is both unrealistic and unhealthy. It leads only to the frustrating, expensive, and sometimes dangerous chemical cycle.

HUNTING FOR BUGS

Insect pests aren't as easy to spot as weeds. Many of them do their dirty work below ground. Others hide in thatch layers. But it's important to find them.

For the soil-dwellers, especially white grubs (beetle larvae), you'll have to look where they live. That means digging out a clump of turf with a spade and searching through the soil for them. Don't be alarmed if you find some. Grubs are common in most lawns, and a few won't do any damage. If you find only three or four per square foot, there's no need to take action.

For other soil- and thatch-dwelling insects, you can try flushing them out. The simplest way is to fill a pump sprayer with 3 tablespoons of dishwashing soap to a gallon of water, or with insecticidal soap diluted as directed on the label. Thoroughly drench a square yard of turf. As the soapy water sinks in, insects will rise to the surface so that you can spot and identify them.

Or you can use the can method. Cut off both ends of a 2-pound coffee can and push one end a few inches into the soil. Fill the can with water, and keep pouring until none drains out. If there are chinch bugs in that area of the lawn, they will float to the surface of the water.

You also can simply get down on your hands and knees, part the grass, and look for bugs at the base of the plants. Whatever method you choose, check the lawn once a month during the growing season. If you don't see more than a dozen bugs in any square foot, generally no action is required. You'll read more about how to determine what constitutes a damaging number of insects in Chapter 8.

For an early warning, it's best to monitor stressed areas where bugs usually occur first. These include sunny dry spots and the edges of the lawn near sidewalks and buildings.

DIAGNOSING DISEASES

Diseases are the most difficult lawn problem to diagnose. Chapter 9 describes disease symptoms. But before turning to it, make sure the problem you're dealing with is really a disease. Diseases usually occur as spots, rings, or patches of discolored and dying grass. But there are many other factors that can cause similar symptoms. Insect damage is one. Dog damage is another. Dying patches can also be caused by gasoline or herbicide spills, burns from lawnmower exhaust, poor drainage, and compacted soils.

Nearly all lawn disease can be traced to fungi. Often you can see the fungus mycelium on the plants, especially on dewy mornings. Damaged areas may appear pinkish or sooty. If fungus is present, it's a sure sign that disease is involved. But if these signs are not present, don't eliminate disease from consideration. The questionnaire on page 184 of Chapter 9 will help you play disease detective.

MONITORING CHART

Your monitoring will go more smoothly if you use a chart like the one below. Use it whenever you check the lawn. If you find problems, make a note of them. When you take action to solve the problem, note the results so that you can continue the successful programs and eliminate the failures.

	Date	Location	Description	Action Taken	Result
Weeds					
Insects					
Diseases					
Thatch					

Diagnosis will also be easier if you keep track of how often you mow, water, and fertilize your lawn.

2

WHICH GRASS SHOULD YOU GROW?

A breeding revolution is sweeping lawns across the country. The world of horticulture has never seen anything like it. New and improved varieties of grass are appearing on the shelves almost too fast to keep up with. And it all benefits the homeowner.

We're asking grasses to do more than ever before, and breeders are delivering. They're turning out new varieties that survive longer without water; grasses that fight off insects and diseases; grasses that handle heat or cold, drought or excess moisture.

These new grasses stay green longer without fertilizers; they grow fast and thick enough to crowd out weeds. Some new grasses thrive in deep shade; others stand up under heavy traffic.

All of the advances haven't necessarily made choosing a grass variety for your lawn any easier. There still isn't one supergrass that can do it all. For now, you have to pick and choose among the best. That means you should know what your conditions are, and what you want from your grass.

WILD AND WOOLLY

This wealth of choices is a relatively recent development. Forty years ago, the selections for a quality lawn pretty much began and ended with Kentucky bluegrass for the North and bermudagrass for the South. But now former ruffian grasses like tall fescue, perennial ryegrass, and bahia are showing up in the finest places; they're holding their own with the best of them for looks, while paving new ground for low-maintenance turf.

In the Middle Ages, only the wealthy could afford a lawn and someone to cut it. Grass seed was not available. Instead, hunks of sod were dug up from pastures and laid out on prepared soil. And that was the lawn.

Until surprisingly recently, most of our lawn grasses were selected from pastures and prairies. Turf experts searched the wild for "sports"—single plants of a species that showed better texture, improved vigor, or other outstanding qualities. They dug up these talented plants and grew them out for seed. The millions of pounds of 'Manhattan' ryegrass sold since 1967 originated from a single plant dug out of Central Park in New York City. 'Merion' Kentucky bluegrass, which turned the turf world on its ear with excellent disease resistance and hardiness, came from a single plant discovered growing on a golf course in Ardmore, Pennsylvania. That's the way all new grass cultivars were developed until the late 1960s.

Now breeders are using hybridization, cloning, and selection to produce grasses our parents could only dream about. And they are looking for grasses that perform well on lawns, not just on golf courses. Traditionally, most of our grass was bred to thrive under intense management, high fertility, low cutting heights, and frequent irrigation—the sort of conditions that prevail on a golf course. When those grasses were sown in the home lawn, the homeowner had to follow a high-maintenance program to keep them healthy and looking good. The emphasis has changed. The new byword is *low* maintenance.

The star grasses today are turf type tall fescues and turf type perennial ryegrasses. Both have their roots in pastures, but they've found a home in our lawns.

COOL OR WARM

Although there are hundreds of species of grass, they can be divided into two camps—cool-season grasses (those that grow best in spring and fall, grow slowly or go dormant during the summer, and stay green into the winter) and warm-season grasses (those that do most of their growing during the hot summer months and turn brown when the weather cools). The former, of course, grow best in the northern states, and the latter are best suited to the southern states. Then there is the gray area, the transition zone, where both types will grow, although neither is at its best.

Cool-season grasses grow best at temperatures of 60° to 75°F. They may go dormant during the hot weather of the summer.

Warm-season grasses are happiest at temperatures of 80° to 95°F. They lose their color and go dormant in the fall.

The border between the lawn camps is the so-called bluegrass line. It runs approximately along the northern borders of North Carolina, Tennessee, Arkansas, Oklahoma, and Texas, through New Mexico and Arizona to the Pacific through the lower part of California. Above the line, bluegrass is the preferred species. Below it, bluegrass won't grow and bermudagrass takes over as the most common species. The United States is further divided into five areas based on climate.

■ *Zone one* is the humid Northeast, which supports Kentucky bluegrass, along with bents, Chewings fescues, improved turf type tall fescues, and improved perennial ryegrasses.

■ *Zone two* is the humid South. The best grasses for this area are bermudagrass, zoysia, and, in certain areas, carpetgrass, centipedegrass, St. Augustinegrass, and bahiagrass.

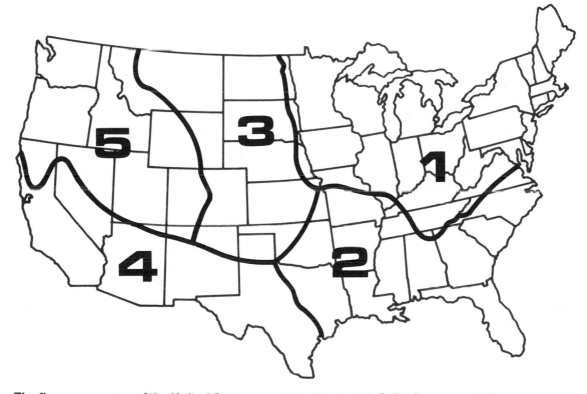

The five grass zones of the United States are: *1*, the Northeast; *2*, the South; *3*, the Plains; *4*, the Southwest; and *5*, the Northwest.

■ *Zone three* is the Great Plains. Bluegrass can be grown there under irrigation. For low maintenance, the best choices are blue gramagrass, buffalograss, and crested wheat grass.

■ *Zone four* is the dry Southwest. It supports bermudagrass and zoysia. Bluegrass and fescues may be grown at high altitudes.

■ *Zone five* is the humid Northwest. The grass choices there are the same as for Zone one: Kentucky bluegrass, bents, fescues, and ryegrass.

rior to common tall fescue, they were hardly suited for turf. In spite of the fact that the early fescues are still occasionally found in seed mixtures, they made lousy lawn grasses.

The blades of these fescues are coarse. Their growth habit is bunching. The plants grow in clumps and do not make a thick sod. That leaves plenty of room for weeds to infiltrate. And they do not mix well with

(continued on page 22)

A TALE OF TALL FESCUE

You might say that tall fescue is the ugly duckling of turfgrasses. One hundred years ago, it started its life in America as a weed. Not until 50 years later was a use found for it, as a forage grass for cattle. Agronomists then went to work, and in 1940 two improved varieties were introduced: 'Alta' and 'Kentucky 31'. Both were used for forage and, in limited amounts, for turfgrass. Like many turfgrasses, 'Alta' and 'Kentucky 31' weren't so much bred as discovered. Plants were picked out of stands of forage grass for their superior qualities, such as winter-hardiness or improved growth habits.

These early fescues had some admirable qualities, especially their strong, fast-growing roots that could dig deeply into the soil, making the grass more drought-tolerant than most. They were also wear-tolerant and formed no thatch. Although those qualities made the selections supe-

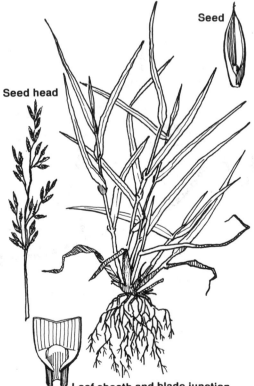

Seed

Seed head

Leaf sheath and blade junction

Tall fescue is a medium- to coarse-textured bunch grass that requires minimal fertilizer.

RATING THE GRASSES

All turfgrass species have their strong points and their shortcomings. The following is a general ranking of species according to their lawn qualities, listed in order of their performance over a range (as fine to coarse, low to high, etc.). However, in some cases the improved varieties of a species will rank higher than indicated.

	Cool-Season	Warm-Season
Texture		
Fine	Red fescue	Improved bermudagrass
	Creeping bentgrass	Zoysiagrass
	Colonial bentgrass	Centipedegrass
	Kentucky bluegrass	Bahiagrass
	Perennial ryegrass	Common bermudagrass
	Turf type tall fescue	Meadow fescue
	—	St. Augustinegrass
Coarse	—	Carpetgrass
Nitrogen Needs		
Low	Red fescue	Bahiagrass
	Tall fescue	Carpetgrass
	Meadow fescue	Centipedegrass
	Perennial ryegrass	Zoysiagrass
	Kentucky bluegrass	St. Augustinegrass
	Colonial bentgrass	Improved bermudagrass
	Creeping bentgrass	Common bermudagrass
High	—	Dichondra

(continued)

RATING THE GRASSES—Continued

	Cool-Season	Warm-Season
Heat Tolerance		
High	—	Zoysiagrass
	—	Improved bermudagrass
	—	Common bermudagrass
	—	Carpetgrass
	—	Centipedegrass
	—	St. Augustinegrass
	—	Bahiagrass
	Tall fescue	—
	—	Dichondra
	Meadow fescue	—
	Kentucky bluegrass	—
	Colonial bentgrass	—
	Red fescue	—
	Ryegrass	—
Low	Creeping bentgrass	—
Cold Tolerance		
High	Kentucky bluegrass	—
	Creeping bentgrass	—
	Colonial bentgrass	—
	Perennial ryegrass	—
	Red fescue	—
	Tall fescue	—
	Meadow fescue	—
	—	Zoysiagrass
	—	Common bermudagrass
	—	Improved bermudagrass
	—	Dichondra
	—	Carpetgrass
	—	Centipedegrass
Low	—	St. Augustinegrass

	Cool-Season	Warm-Season
Drought Tolerance		
High	Tall fescue	Improved bermudagrass
	Red fescue	Zoysiagrass
	Kentucky bluegrass	Common bermudagrass
	Perennial ryegrass	Bahiagrass
	Meadow fescue	St. Augustinegrass
	Colonial bentgrass	Centipedegrass
	Creeping bentgrass	Carpetgrass
Low	—	Dichondra
Compacted Soil Tolerance		
High	Tall fescue	—
	—	Improved bermudagrass
	—	Common bermudagrass
	—	Zoysiagrass
	Kentucky bluegrass	—
	Perennial ryegrass	—
	Meadow fescue	—
	—	St. Augustinegrass
	Red fescue	—
	—	Dichondra
	Colonial bentgrass	—
Low	Creeping bentgrass	—
Wear Tolerance		
High	Tall fescue	Zoysiagrass
	Perennial ryegrass	Bermudagrass
	Meadow fescue	Bahiagrass
	Kentucky bluegrass	St. Augustinegrass
	Red fescue	Carpetgrass
	Colonial bentgrass	Centipedegrass
Low	Creeping bentgrass	—

(continued)

RATING THE GRASSES—Continued

	Cool-Season	Warm-Season
Rate of Establishment		
Fast	Perennial ryegrass	Bermudagrass
	Creeping bentgrass	St. Augustinegrass
	Meadow fescue	Bahiagrass
	Tall fescue	Centipedegrass
	Kentucky bluegrass	Carpetgrass
	Bentgrasses	Zoysiagrass
Slow	Red fescue	—
Thatching Potential		
Low	Tall fescue	Bahiagrass
	Perennial ryegrass	Carpetgrass
	Fine fescues	Centipedegrass
	Kentucky bluegrass	Zoysiagrass
	Colonial bentgrass	St. Augustinegrass
High	Creeping bentgrass	Bermudagrass

other turfgrasses. Add to that their sensitivity to cold temperatures, and it's no wonder they never caught on as turfgrasses. But all that has changed.

By 1985, the few fescue varieties had proliferated to at least 25, with the numbers increasing rapidly. The new turf type tall fescues are built tough. They carry the species drought resistance, making them the most drought-tolerant of any cool-season grasses. This explains why they are especially attractive for the transition zone, where water is often at a premium. They also have good shade tolerance, which bermudagrass and Kentucky bluegrass lack.

The new fescues are tough and can stand up to a lot of traffic, but they've also put on a pretty face. These new varieties have softer leaves and a lower growing habit than the original tall fescues. That means they are easier to mow, and require mowing less frequently.

Turf type tall fescue does not require heavy feeding. New varieties offer a rich green color without heavy amounts of nitrogen. They show resistance to such diseases as brown patch, leaf spot, and stem rust, and at least one variety, 'Apache', fights off insects.

TALL FESCUE FACTS

Turf type tall fescue is a cool-season grass that is at its best where conditions are too warm for most cool-season grasses and too cool for warm-season grasses. It is well adapted to a wide range of soil conditions, including acid soil in a range of pH 5.5 to 6.5.

To establish a lawn, use 8 pounds of seed per 1,000 square feet. This seeding rate will produce the optimum spread of 13 plants per square inch. Tall fescue does not mix well with other grasses.

Turf type tall fescue is not a heavy feeder. In the North, where the growing season is short, it requires only 2 pounds of nitrogen per 1,000 square feet. The fertilizer works best if applied in the fall. In the South, where the growing season is longer, the grass will require up to 4 pounds of nitrogen per 1,000 square feet, applied in the spring. Mow at 2 to 4 inches.

THE BEST OF THE PACK

The Lawn Institute, a seedmen's association, has singled out six varieties of turf type tall fescue for recognition. They are 'Apache', 'Clemfine', 'Rebel', 'Houndog', 'Falcon', and 'Mustang'.

'Apache' is low growing and dark green, with resistance to leaf spot and brown patch. It is also somewhat resistant to damage from weevils, billbugs, and sod webworms because it hosts endophyte fungi (see Insects Avoid These Grasses on page 26). It will not form thatch. As is typical of tall fescues, it does not mix well with other species, but it may be mixed with 5 percent improved Kentucky bluegrass for a finer turf. The recommended mowing height is 1½ to 2 inches.

'Clemfine', developed at Clemson University in South Carolina, has a coarse leaf texture similar to that of 'Kentucky 31' tall fescue and grows in bunches, but tests have shown it to be more persistent while maintaining a solid turf stand under heat and drought. It has proven its ability to withstand shade from Texas to New Jersey. The best mowing height is 2 to 4 inches.

'Rebel' grows nearly twice as dense as 'Kentucky 31' tall fescue. Its narrow leaf width is 30 percent less coarse than that of 'KY31'. In trials, 'Rebel' outscored all other tall fescues in overall quality ratings. It is resistant to net blotch.

'Houndog' is known for its deep green color. It rated highest for color in a competition with 15 other tall fescues. It's a low-growing grass, and does not need mowing as often as some. The recommended mowing height is 1½ to 3 inches. 'Houndog' has resistance to net blotch and brown patch.

'Falcon' has fairly fine leaves and forms a dense, persistent turf with a medium-green color. It's a good grass for heavily used home lawns. 'Falcon' shows disease resistance to brown patch and net blotch.

It tolerates a soil pH range of 4.5 to 8. The preferred mowing height for 'Falcon' is 2 to 3 inches, although it will tolerate a cut as low as 1½ inches.

'Mustang' was released from germ plasm developed at Rutgers University in New Jersey. Its parents include plants collected from old turf in the Mid-Atlantic states as well as hybrids of tall fescue, meadow fescue, and perennial ryegrass. Selection was based on dark green color, soft leaves, and resistance to drechslera leaf blight. Mustang is also resistant to net blotch and brown patch.

PERENNIAL RYEGRASS PAYS OFF

You might call perennial ryegrass the Cinderella of turfgrasses. For years it has been a hardworking stepsister. Like tall fescue, it started out as a pasture grass, and has been counted on to feed livestock in Great Britain since the seventeenth century. Through years of selection, good short-lived hay types were developed and became widely used in the southern and northwestern United States.

But although they performed well enough in pastures, perennial ryegrasses were not the stuff that great lawns are made of. They were stemmy, coarse-leaved, and short-lived. Nevertheless, they were often found in cheap grass mixtures. Why? The ryegrasses are prolific seed-producers, and the seed was inexpensive. And early ryegrass did have some good qualities. It ger-

minated and established itself rapidly — so rapidly that when mixed with Kentucky bluegrass, it could take over a lawn before the bluegrass got its footing.

Then, in the 1960s, 'Manhattan' and 'Pennfine' ushered in a new era in ryegrass. The disease resistance of these varieties caused them to become immediate sensations. And they looked like they belonged in a lawn. The two varieties began showing up in the finest of mixes.

When turf breeders saw what was possible, they got serious about perennial ryegrass, and soon introduced other improved varieties to the market. Perennial ryegrass made another great leap with the discovery that some species hosted endophytes. These are fungi that had troubled cattlemen and farmers by producing neuro-

PERENNIAL RYEGRASSES FOR THE NORTH

Some old perennial ryegrasses like 'Linn' and 'Caravelle' get battered in the winter. They may limp through to spring with up to 40 percent of the grass injured, even in not-so-frigid areas like New Jersey. But several of the new, improved perennial ryegrasses showed no winter injury in New Jersey trials. They are 'Blazer', 'Yorktown II', 'Belle', 'Pennant', 'Fiesta', 'Diplomat', 'Dasher', 'Omega', 'Regal', and 'Manhattan'.

toxins that can cause serious illness in grazing cattle. But scientists discovered that endophyte-infected grasses had one-fifth as many weevils as ordinary grasses. Later studies showed these grasses repelled bluegrass billbug, sod webworm, and other insects.

Researchers realized they had found a grass that bugs refused to eat. They discovered that endophytes were passed on to the next grass generation through the seed. Suddenly, a slew of insect-resistant ryegrasses hit the market. They not only fight insects, but are fine-leaved and persistent, with a deeper green color. They have improved heat and cold tolerance, and will grow in up to 60 percent shade. They're easier to mow and take well to low mowing. Many have multiple disease resistance. And they still retain the quick coverage ability and relatively low price of their ancestors.

Perennial ryegrass should be seeded at 4 to 8 pounds per 1,000 square feet. Fertilize at 2 pounds of nitrogen per 1,000 square feet once a year. The recommended cutting height is 1½ to 2 inches.

THE BEST OF THE PERENNIAL RYEGRASSES

Here are some of the new turf type perennial ryegrasses recommended by the Lawn Institute.

'**All Star**' is one of the bug-fighting newcomers. It repels sod webworm, weevils, webworms, billbugs, and other insects. It also carries resistance to leaf spot, large brown patch, and crown rust. 'All Star' is a fine-textured ryegrass with dark green color. It performs best in full sun.

'**Omega**' perennial ryegrass is touted for its cold tolerance, and has gotten high marks as far north as the University of Vermont. 'Omega' survived New Jersey winters unscathed, while other ryegrasses suffered up to 48 percent damage. It also

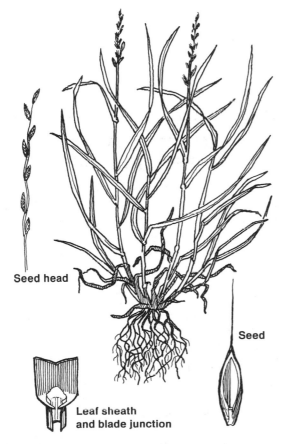

Seed head

Seed

Leaf sheath and blade junction

Perennial ryegrass is a medium-textured, spreading grass that germinates quickly.

TOUGH TURF

If you really *use* your lawn, for picnicking, playing volleyball, and so on, you need a grass that can stand up to heavy wear and traffic. Your best choice is to look to varieties that were developed for use on athletic fields. 'Manhattan' and 'Manhattan II' perennial ryegrasses are two good varieties.

Tough grass tends to have a low crown, tough leaves, and the ability to bounce back from wear.

ready for mowing in 21 days. You can walk on it in five weeks.

'**Repell**' was developed specifically for insect resistance. Its resident endophytes make the grass unappetizing to cutworms, sod webworms, armyworms, billbug larvae, Argentine stem weevil larvae, and chinch bugs. It also shows good resistance to brown blight and brown patch, and some tolerance to fusarium patch. 'Repell' is a leafy, persistent strain with the ability to grow in moderate shade. It scored first in an overall quality trial of 29 perennial ryegrasses.

'**Pennant**' is low-growing, so it requires less mowing. "Medium" is the operative

shows improved resistance to winter brown blight disease, brown patch, red thread, fusarium patch, and snow mold.

'**Manhattan II**' is the son of 'Manhattan', the famous ryegrass that started all the fuss. It may be tough for children to live up to the reputation of famous parents, but 'Manhattan II' does that and then some. It's an entirely new variety, with the following improved characteristics: greater density, darker green foliage, finer leaf texture, heat and drought tolerance, shade adaptation, and resistance to brown patch, crown rust, and stem rust. 'Manhattan II' can be used alone or mixed in equal amounts with Kentucky bluegrass and fine fescue for best appearance. 'Manhattan II' grows well in compacted soils, making it a fine grass for areas with heavy traffic. The new 'Manhattan' hasn't sacrificed the ability to germinate quickly. It comes up in 7 days, and will be

INSECTS AVOID THESE GRASSES

If insects are troubling your lawn, you can plant a variety that they'll stay away from. New perennial ryegrasses and at least one turf type tall fescue have been bred for increased content of endophytes, a fungus that bugs find distasteful. These grasses will repel Argentine stem weevil, cherry aphid, greenbug aphid, armyworm, billbug larva, cutworm, and sod webworm. The resistant varieties are 'Apache' tall fescue and the following perennial ryegrasses: 'Repell', 'Citation II', 'Pennant', 'Regal', 'Prelude', 'Cowboy', 'All Star', and 'Premier'. These all have high endophyte levels. The following varieties have moderate endophyte levels: 'Palmer', 'Derby', 'Dasher', 'Pennfine', 'Delray', and 'Linn'.

word for 'Pennant'. Its texture is medium fine, its growth is medium-high density, and its color is medium dark. 'Pennant' is both heat- and cold-tolerant. Its middle-of-the-pack nature means the grass has wide geographic and climatic adaptability. It scored well in trials across the country for such traits as winter-hardiness and resistance to brown patch and red thread. 'Pennant' also shows resistance to winter brown blight and crown rust.

'Citation II' is called a "hard-use" turfgrass. It has good seedling vigor and stands up to traffic and wear. This variety looks good, too. The leaves are fine, and plants are dense, with a dark blue-green color. 'Citation II' also has a high endophyte level, so it resists insect damage. It is

---

PERENNIAL RYEGRASS PICKS

The National Turfgrass Evaluation Program rates grass species for several qualities. Here is a look at the best-scoring perennial ryegrasses, with the highest-scoring varieties listed first in each category.

Spring Greenup: 'Palmer', 'Premier', 'Gator', 'Ranger', 'Yorktown'

Color: 'Gator', 'Blazer', 'Manhattan II', 'Palmer', 'Prelude'

Leaf Texture: 'Manhattan II', 'Barry', 'Gator', 'Crown', 'Diplomat'

Summer Density: 'Barry', 'Gator', 'Premier', 'Derby', 'Fiesta'

Frost Tolerance: 'Maverick', 'Adventure', 'Arid', 'Festorina', 'Finelawn I'

Slow Growth: 'Jaguar', 'Apache', 'Olympic', 'Bonanza', 'Adventure'

The program also rates varieties for overall quality for each of the states and provinces where trials are held. Here are the 1986 results.

British Columbia: 'Gator', 'Derby', 'Manhattan II'

California: 'Palmer', 'Tara', 'Citation II'

Illinois: 'Yorktown II', 'Diplomat', 'Gator'

Iowa: 'Citation II', 'Palmer', 'Ranger'

Kentucky: 'Gator', 'Repell', 'Tara'

Maryland (Beltsville): 'Palmer', 'Repell', 'Blazer'

Maryland (Silver Spring): 'Derby', 'All Star', 'Pennant'

Massachusetts: 'Ranger', 'Pennfine', 'Ovation'

Missouri: 'Blazer', 'Fiesta', 'Gator'

Nebraska: 'Manhattan II', 'Gator', 'Tara'

New Jersey: 'Blazer', 'Palmer', 'Citation II'

New York: 'All Star', 'Elka', 'Crown'

North Carolina: 'Pennant', 'Acclaim', 'Citation II'

Oregon: 'Citation II', 'Manhattan II', 'Birdie II'

Rhode Island: 'Crown', 'Repell', 'Citation II'

Virginia: 'Regal', 'Prelude', 'Palmer'

Washington: 'Palmer', 'Manhattan II', 'Repell'

resistant to brown patch, red thread, and dollar spot.

'Prelude' is a good all-around turfgrass, adapted to many areas of the country. It has heat and drought tolerance and good winter-hardiness, especially on well-drained soils. Combine that with resistance to crown rust, large brown patch, and winter leaf spot, and you have one of the more persistent perennial ryegrasses. 'Prelude' is a leafy, moderately dense, low-growing, fine-textured turfgrass with a rich, dark green color. It performs well both in full sun and in light to moderate shade.

KENTUCKY BLUEGRASS IS KING

Kentucky bluegrass is the king of turfgrasses. For most of the country, nothing makes a better lawn. It can stand the heat and drought of the middle South, the frigid winters of New England, and the humidity of the Northwest. And it does more than tolerate these conditions. With its fine-textured, deep green blades, its spreading habit, and its quick sod-forming ability, it makes the kind of lawn neighbors envy.

But not all Kentucky bluegrass is perfect. There is quite a difference among varieties and strains of the species. The cheapest is called common Kentucky bluegrass, and you'll often find it in inexpensive mixtures. It is the offspring of grass selected from the wild, not much changed from colonial times. Over the years, strains of common bluegrass have been selected for their better

qualities and named as varieties. Those still available include 'Delta', 'Kenblue', 'Newport', 'Park', and 'South Dakota'.

Then along came 'Merion'. Discovered growing in the wild and released in the early 1950s, 'Merion' gave breeders and turfgrass experts a glimpse of what a Kentucky bluegrass could be.

The fine-textured, rich green blades of Kentucky bluegrass make it the most favored species for good looks.

'Merion' was hailed as a miracle grass because of its resistance to drechslera leaf spot and crown rot, two diseases that ravaged common Kentucky bluegrass across the country. Suddenly, the best lawn grass was even better. 'Merion' became a sensation, and millions of pounds of it were sow from coast to coast. But it didn't take long to discover that 'Merion' had its own shortcomings — susceptibility to two previously minor bluegrass diseases, ophiobolus and stripe smut.

'Merion' was followed by 'Fylking', a Swedish development with tolerance to melting out and stripe smut, along with resistance or tolerance to seven other diseases: leaf rust, stem rust, crown rust, dollar spot, red thread, fusarium blight, and fusarium patch.

Then, in the late 1960s, researchers at Rutgers University developed a reliable method for hybridizing Kentucky bluegrass so that desirable characteristics could be built into a bluegrass variety. Before long, 'Merion' and 'Fylking' were joined by more than 80 varieties, most with resistance to more than one disease. The result? Kentucky bluegrasses can be tailored to regions and local diseases, and the king extends his kingdom.

Although some of the new Kentucky bluegrasses are the result of hybridization ('Adelphi', 'America', and 'Eclipse', for example), many were selected from screening trials, lawns, golf courses, and parks throughout the country. Their regional origin gives some clue to their adaptability. They're bound to grow well in the areas where they were discovered.

THE BEST OF BLUEGRASS

The following 14 varieties have been selected by the Lawn Institute for special recognition.

'Adelphi' is known primarily for maintaining its deep green color throughout the season. It is a low-growing cultivar, so it takes well to close clipping. 'Adelphi' has resistance to just about every disease imaginable, including stripe smut, rusts, dollar spot, red thread, and fusarium. It is well adapted across the country.

'America' is also low-growing and leafy, so it produces a thick sod. It has resistance to stripe smut and tolerance of leaf spots, powdery mildew, fusarium blight, and rust.

'Arboretum' was selected from old lawns and pastures in Missouri and neighboring states. It is an erect-growing type, well suited for low-maintenance lawns.

'Eclipse' grows well in shade and produces medium-textured turf of good density and vigor. It is resistant to a wide range of diseases, including stripe smut, rusts, fusarium blight, and fusarium patch.

'Fylking', developed in Sweden, is noted for its good color from early spring through late autumn. It has fine-textured foliage and stays leafy during the late spring reproductive cycle. 'Fylking' is also noted for disease resistance to leaf spot, stripe smut, rusts, fusarium blight, and fusarium patch.

'Glade' was selected from an old lawn in Albany, New York. It is known for its shade tolerance and its excellent resistance to rusts, powdery mildew, and smuts. This grass grows slowly and requires less mowing, but it is aggressive in preventing weed infestations.

'**Merit**' comes from southern California. It is dark blue-green and produces a dense turf that persists over a wide range of environmental conditions. It is moderately low-growing with a medium-coarse texture, and is known for its seedling vigor. 'Merit' has been the top-rated cultivar in Northeast and Midwest trials. It is resistant to leaf spot, stripe smut, rusts, dollar spot, red thread, and fusarium blight.

'**Monopoly**', developed in Holland, has excellent heat tolerance. This vigorous lawn grass germinates rapidly and establishes well. It has medium-green foliage with medium texture. It has rated well in Northeast and transitional South trials, and is resistant to stripe smut, rusts, red thread, fusarium blight, and fusarium patch.

'**Nassau**' produces a moderately low-growing turf of medium density. It is known for its early spring color and its resistance to a broad range of diseases, including leaf spot, stripe smut, rusts, red thread, dollar spot, fusarium blight, and fusarium patch. Nassau has been the top-rated cultivar in transitional South and Midwest trials.

'**Nugget**' was selected from turf in Alaska, and is noted for its very dense, compact, low-growing characteristics. This grass takes close mowing and some shade, and shows good resistance to leaf spot, powdery mildew, and leaf rust. 'Nugget' has been the top-rated cultivar in northern Midwest trials; it is well suited for lawns in the northern United States.

'**Ram 1**' was selected from a golf putting green in Kennebunk Beach, Maine. It is leafy, low-growing, and takes close mowing well. It has rich, dark green foliage and good disease resistance to stripe smut, powdery mildew, rusts, and fusarium blight. 'Ram 1' has won top ratings in the National Turfgrass Evaluation Program and in Canadian turf trials.

'**Rugby**' originated in a park in Peoria, Illinois. It is a dense, aggressive, vigorously spreading grass that is also known for tolerance to close mowing. 'Rugby' keeps its strong color well into autumn. It is resistant to diseases including leaf spot, stripe smut, rusts, dollar spot, red thread, and fusarium blight.

'**Sydsport**' was developed in Sweden, where it is often used on athletic fields. It is known for wear tolerance and dense sod. Its light green blades are medium wide. 'Sydsport' is resistant to leaf spot, stripe smut, powdery mildew, rusts, dollar spot, and fusarium blight.

'**Touchdown**' comes from a golf course on Long Island. It is very aggressive, with medium-textured, dark green foliage. It is known for its ability to drive out annual bluegrass when mowed close. 'Touchdown' grows well in moderate shade and has good resistance to leaf spot, stripe smut, powdery mildew, dollar spot, red thread, and fusarium blight.

OTHER BLUES

Canada bluegrass is a fine-textured, sod-forming perennial that can be recognized by its flattened stems. It does not recover well from mowing, and makes a

BLUE RIBBONS FOR BLUEGRASSES

With more than 80 varieties of Kentucky bluegrass on the market, choosing the right one for your lawn can be a challenge. Many of them are regionally adapted: What works in New York might not make it in Washington. But the U.S. Department of Agriculture is doing its part to ease the confusion. The National Turfgrass Evaluation Program, sponsored by the USDA, evaluates turfgrass varieties at 37 test gardens in 22 states. The cultivars are rated for insect and disease resistance, drought tolerance, seasonal appearance, density, sod strength, and leaf texture. The USDA names the strongest overall varieties, both nationwide and for the state where the tests were held.

In 1986, 'Midnight' scored highest overall, followed, in order, by 'Blacksburg', 'Rugby', 'Asset', and 'Tendos'. Here is how the grasses ranked by specific quality, with the best variety listed first.

Spring Greenup: 'Midnight', 'Amazon', 'America', 'Challenger', 'Dawn'

Color: 'Midnight', 'Eclipse', 'Destiny', 'Glade', 'Bristol'

Leaf Texture: 'Kenblue', 'Joy', 'S.D. Certified', 'Cynthia', 'Amazon'

Seedling Vigor: 'Monopoly', 'Somerset', 'Parade', 'S.D. Certified', 'Welcome'

Spring Density: 'America', 'Classic', 'Dawn', 'Loft's 1757', 'Asset'

Summer Density: 'America', 'Blacksburg', 'Challenger', 'Sydsport', 'Baron'

Drought Tolerance: 'Able I', 'Amazon', 'America', 'Aquila', 'Aspen'

Sod Strength: 'Sydsport', 'America', 'Aspen', 'Glade', 'Welcome'

The state-by-state results are as follows. Again, the best variety for each state or province is listed first.

British Columbia: 'Sydsport', 'Trenton', 'America'

California: 'Classic', 'Glade', 'Trenton'

D.C.: 'Ikone', 'Glade', 'Julia'

Georgia: 'Baron', 'Cheri', 'Challenger'

Idaho: 'Midnight', 'Georgetown', 'Rugby'

Indiana: 'Mystic', 'America', 'Somerset'

Kansas: 'Midnight', 'Bristol', 'Ikone'

Kentucky: 'Blacksburg', 'Classic', 'America'

Maryland: 'Midnight', 'Blacksburg', 'Ikone'

Minnesota: 'Mystic', 'Rugby', 'Princeton'

Missouri: 'America', 'Dawn', 'Harmony'

New Jersey: 'Midnight', 'Crystal', 'America'

New Mexico: 'Midnight', 'Classic', 'Julia'

North Carolina: 'Baron', 'Merit', 'Victa'

Ohio: 'Midnight', 'America', 'Challenger'

Oregon: 'Blacksburg', 'Challenger', 'Midnight'

Rhode Island: 'Blacksburg', 'Liberty', 'Amazon'

Virginia: 'Midnight', 'Victa', 'Blacksburg'

Washington: 'Sydsport', 'Cheri', 'Ikone'

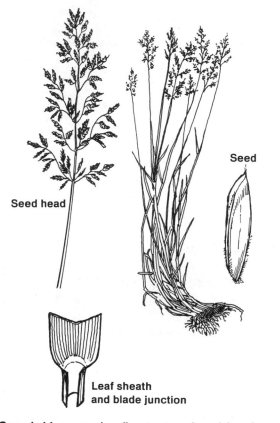

Seed head

Seed

Leaf sheath
and blade junction

Canada bluegrass is a fine-textured, sod-forming
species, useful only in soils too dry or acidic
for Kentucky bluegrass.

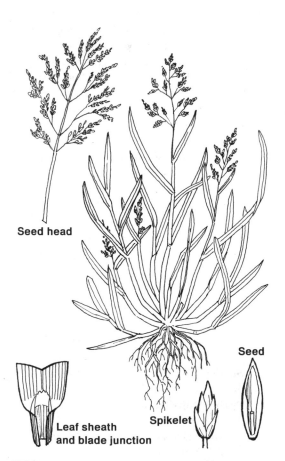

Seed head

Seed

Spikelet

Leaf sheath
and blade junction

Although fine-textured and sod-forming, rough
bluegrass should be planted only in moist,
shady locations.

thin, scrawny turf. It may be useful on soils that are too dry, too acid, or too deficient in nutrients for Kentucky bluegrass, but it is not recommended for high-quality lawns.

Rough bluegrass is a fine-textured, sod-forming perennial that spreads by stolons. Though it is found in many seed mixes, it shines only in moist, shady locations. 'Sabre' is the only improved variety.

rapid germination (5 to 12 days) and seedling establishment, they make a good nurse crop when mixed with the slower Kentucky bluegrass. Because they have good disease resistance (except in the southern part of their range), they give lawns better resistance when they're mixed with other grasses. And they are excellent for overseeding poor lawns to improve turf quality.

THE FAIR-HAIRED FESCUES

Fine fescues have the finest leaves of any lawn grass. Their upright growth habit creates a high degree of uniformity for a good, even-looking lawn. But despite their good looks, they are not prima donnas. They work hard. Fine fescues are the most shade-tolerant of all cool-season lawn grasses. They stand heat and cold well and are also drought-tolerant. Like Kentucky bluegrass, they enter a summer dormancy when water is withheld.

Fescue leaves are not succulent, and they do not bruise easily. That makes them wear-resistant and a good choice for play areas. It doesn't take a lot of feeding to get all of these qualities — only 1 pound of nitrogen per 1,000 square feet. You won't find a grass that's less hungry. Fine fescues grow well in well-drained, infertile soils and withstand a pH as low as 5.

Because of all these fine qualities, fine fescues make terrific stand-alone lawns. They all shine in mixtures, too, blending well with other species. Because of their

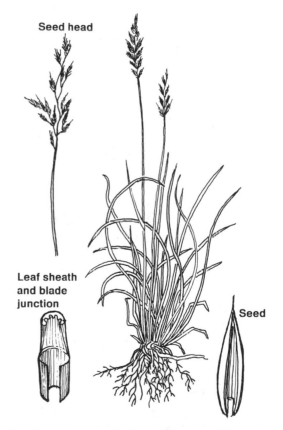

Seed head

Leaf sheath and blade junction

Seed

Fine fescues have the finest-textured blades of all northern grasses. They also germinate quickly and stand a lot of wear and tear.

When used alone, they should be seeded at a rate of 4 pounds per 1,000 square feet.

Like Kentucky bluegrass, perennial ryegrass, and tall fescue, fine fescues have come a long way in a short time. Those introduced since the 1960s show startling improvement over the old common varieties such as 'Cascade' and 'Pennlawn' Chewings fescues (Chewings fescues are discussed below). They adapt well to nearly any mowing regime, and are a good choice both on seldom-used roadsides and golf course fairways, where they are clipped at ½ inch. When grown in the shade, they need particularly little maintenance— mowing at 2 inches and a single fall feeding.

Fine fescues as a group are somewhat resistant to many lawn diseases, but they may be injured by red thread, pink patch, and leaf spot. They can be damaged by all common turfgrass insects.

MEET THE FINE FESCUES

There are three types of fine fescue available: red or creeping fescue, Chewings fescue, and hard fescue. Improved varieties within each type are very similar.

Red fescue is a sod-forming perennial that spreads through short rhizomes. It is especially good for cool, humid regions of the United States, where it grows well on acidic poor soil, but it does not take to wet conditions. Red fescue is subject to severe disease damage in the South. Favored varieties include 'Dawson', 'Flyer', 'Fortress', 'Pennlawn', 'Ensylva', and 'Ruby'. They are all resistant to red thread.

THE FINEST FINE FESCUES

The National Turfgrass Evaluation Program picked the best fine fescues from the 47 it tested in 1986. They are listed below in order of preference.

Spring Greenup: 'Reliant', 'ST-2', 'Biljart', 'Estica', 'Weekend'

Color: 'Scaldis', 'ST-2', 'Aurora', 'Valda', 'Bighorn'

Leaf Texture: 'Banner', 'Beauty', 'Victory', 'Flyer', 'Scaldis'

Summer Density: 'Biljart', 'Scaldis', 'ST-2', 'Valda', 'Waldina'

The program also rated varieties for overall quality in each of the states where trials are held.

California: 'Waldina', 'Scaldis', 'ST-2'

Idaho: 'Ceres', 'Reliant', 'Aurora'

Illinois: 'Enjoy', 'Shadow', 'Aurora'

Kansas: 'Bighorn', 'Reliant', 'Aurora'

Kentucky: 'Biljart', 'Bighorn', 'Aurora'

Maryland: 'Ceres', 'Ruby', 'Flyer'

Nebraska: 'Enjoy', 'Flyer', 'Jamestown'

New Jersey: 'Spartan', 'Reliant', 'ST-2'

New York: 'Enjoy', 'Koket', 'Atlanta'

North Carolina: 'Spartan', 'Reliant', 'Aurora'

Oregon: 'Aurora', 'Bighorn', 'ST-2'

Virginia: 'Aurora', 'Biljart', 'Waldina'

Washington: 'Reliant', 'Scaldis', 'Enjoy'

Chewings fescue is similar to red fescue, but it is a bunch grass with a more erect growth habit and no rhizomes. It also stands shade better. Improved varieties include 'Agram' (with resistance to dollar spot), 'Atlanta' (resistant to red thread), and 'Waldorf' (also resists red thread). 'Jamestown' (resistant to fusarium patch) and 'Banner' (resistant to dollar spot) have better heat tolerance than older varieties, and 'Shadow' is a new cultivar with improved resistance to powdery mildew.

Hard fescue is non-spreading bunch grass that's favored mainly for its deep green color, but it is fairly short-lived, and until recently was found primarily in cheap lawn grass mixtures. Now, improved varieties have come along, and hard fescues can be very useful on infertile but well-drained soils, in low-maintenance turfs, and in shade. 'Aurora', 'Biljart', 'Scaldis', 'Tournament', 'Reliant', and 'Waldina' are improved varieties. They have better heat tolerance than Chewings fescues and good resistance to red thread, leaf spot, and dollar spot.

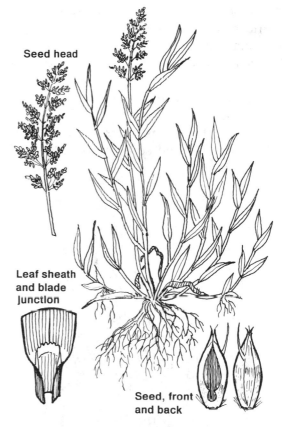

Seed head

Leaf sheath and blade junction

Seed, front and back

Bentgrass can make a beautiful lawn *only* with excessive fertilizer and chemicals. It doesn't belong in the home lawn.

BENTGRASSES DON'T BELONG

The bentgrasses are fine-textured, sod-forming perennials. They are the stuff that putting greens are made of. Twenty years ago they might have been thought of as the epitome of grasses. Today, they really don't belong in the home lawn. That's because bentgrasses are high-maintenance items. There's no way around it. To keep them looking good, you have to mow and water constantly. All that pampering leads to diseases, which call for doses of fungicides. The bentgrasses don't even mix well with low-maintenance grasses. They are so aggressive that they force the other grasses out.

Colonial bentgrass is sometimes found in northern seed mixes, but it tends to dominate other grasses in the mix. It may be useful because it persists on acid soils that will not support Kentucky bluegrass.

Creeping bentgrass thrives in poor, wet soils.

Velvet bentgrass grows on infertile, adequately aerated soils and will tolerate partial shade.

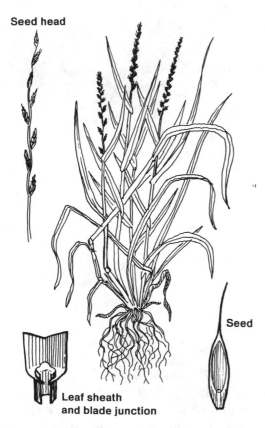

Annual ryegrass is usually coarse-textured. Though quick to germinate, a hard frost will kill it.

Redtop is a coarse, sod-forming perennial member of the bent family. It establishes well on poor and acid soils in the cooler regions of the country. But redtop is not the kind of grass you build a lawn around, because it becomes stemmy and coarse-textured, and dies under close mowing. Nevertheless, it can be useful as a temporary grass.

UNWELCOME GRASSES

Many cool-season grasses are used for forage or soil stabilization, but have no place in the home lawn. Still, you may find them in cheap grass mixtures. Stay away from the following:

Annual (Italian) ryegrass is an annual bunch grass, ranging from fine to coarse. Its texture is determined by sowing rate — coarse-textured when sown thinly, but fine-textured at heavy seeding rates. It is overused in grass mixtures; although its quick germination suits it for temporary lawns in the North, annual ryegrass freezes out over winter and will leave bare patches in the lawn if it comprises more than 20 percent of a mix. It may also be used as an overseeded winter grass in the South, where it dies over the summer.

Velvet grass's coarse texture and bunching habit make it unsuitable for turf.

Orchard grass is a coarse, perennial bunch grass and a troublesome weed in turf.

Reed canarygrass is not suitable for turf because of long, scaly rhizomes and a bunching habit.

Timothy is a coarse, cool-season perennial bunch grass, and is considered a weed in lawns and turf.

Annual bluegrass is an annual bunch grass with a low-growing, tufted habit that makes it unattractive in lawns.

THE HEAT IS ON

Southern lawn owners play by a different set of rules. When it comes to variety selection, they're under a big handicap. Compared to cool-season grasses, varieties suited to warmer climates offer relatively few improved choices. And these few cannot be seeded, but must be started vegetatively through sprigs or sod. That's because most of them produce either sterile or very little seed. A final strike against them: Most species do not mix well with one another as do northern species. Consequently, southern lawns are usually monocultures — all bermudagrass, for example. This increases the chances of a lawn being completely wiped out by disease. To compound the problem, few southern grasses have good disease resistance.

As cool-season grasses are bred with more heat and drought tolerance, they're finding their way to northern areas of the South. In the meantime, breeders are concentrating on improving southern grasses. One improved seeded bermudagrass has just come onto the market. Others are sure to follow.

BERMUDAGRASS

Bermudagrass is to the South what Kentucky bluegrass is to the North. It's everywhere. People depend on it for a turf that doesn't need tender care. It's a coarse to fine, sod-forming perennial that spreads by stolons and rhizomes. The grass is so invasive that it is a serious weed in some areas. However, its vigor means that it establishes quickly, forcing weeds out.

Bermudagrass grows throughout the warmer regions of the United States and into the Midwest and New England. But it turns off-color in cool weather and brown after frost. And while dormant during winter, it may be invaded by weeds. It is a tough, low-maintenance grass, growing on poor soils from heavy clay to deep sand, but it needs high nitrogen levels (monthly feedings of 1 pound of nitrogen per 1,000 square feet) for good-quality turf. In humid regions, it is drought-tolerant. Bermudagrasses can be clipped at heights from ½ to 1½ inches.

Common bermudagrass is the type you'll find in most southern lawns. With one recent exception, it is the only type that can be propagated from seed. To make good turf, it must be fertilized heavily and mowed closely and frequently. And although it's drought-resistant, it needs water in extended periods of dry weather to maintain a good appearance. Seed-grown Bermuda is often more sensitive to severe heat or winter damage during its first year than some of the hybrids. And there is no assurance of uniformity of color or texture when this lawn grass is grown from seed.

To establish a common bermudagrass lawn, sow seed at a rate of 2 to 3 pounds per 1,000 square feet in April, May, or June if the area can be kept well watered.

'**U-3**' is a strain of common Bermuda that was selected from a lawn in Savannah, Georgia. It has finer leaves and stems than common bermudagrass, and produces an excellent turf. It usually turns green earlier in the spring and stays green later in the fall. 'U-3' has many slender runners with leaves distributed along their length. It is very winter-hardy and disease-resistant, but doesn't rank as one of the more wear-resistant strains. It needs frequent mowing to keep it ½ to 1¼ inches tall. On the minus side, this strain spreads more slowly and is more susceptible to spring dead spot than common bermudagrass.

'**Guymon**' is a new seeded variety, developed in Oklahoma. It shows improved texture over common types.

'**Numex S-1**', developed at the University of New Mexico, was created by crossing improved clones. The resulting seed-grown variety grows and looks better than common bermudagrass. It has medium texture and density, and good spring and summer color.

HIGH-CLASS HYBRID BERMUDAS

Hybrid bermudagrasses have been getting a lot of attention lately, but most are intended for high-maintenance golf course fairways. They can't be started from seed. All must be started from sprigs. They require fertilizing every four to six weeks from mid-April to mid-August, with up to 2 pounds of nitrogen per 1,000 square feet at each application. They should be cut at ¾ to 1 inch every five to ten days.

'**Sunturf**' is an improved variety introduced from South Africa. It produces few seed heads and is denser and more attractive than common bermudagrass. The vari-

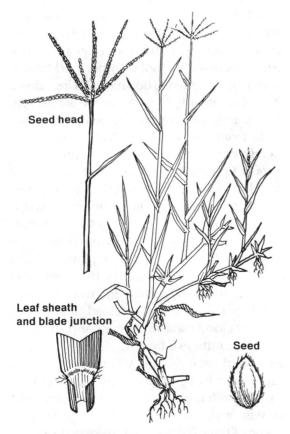

Seed head

Leaf sheath and blade junction

Seed

Bermudagrass texture ranges from coarse to fine, depending on variety. It spreads quickly by stolons and rhizomes.

ety is tolerant of cold, and remains green a bit longer than usual in the fall. It is vegetatively propagated.

THE BEST BERMUDAS

The 1986 National Turfgrass Evaluation trials judged the following bermudagrasses best.

Overall: 'Tifway II', 'Tifway', 'Tifgreen'

Color: 'Texturf 10', 'Tifway II', 'Tifgreen'

Leaf Texture: 'Tifgreen', 'Tifway II', 'Tifway'

Seedling Vigor: 'Guymon', 'Midiron', 'Vamont'

Summer Density: 'Tifgreen', 'Texturf 10', 'Tifway'

Spread: 'Arizona Common', 'Tifgreen', 'Vamont'

Here's a list of the best choices by state.

California (Riverside): 'Tifway', 'Tifway II', 'Tifgreen'

California (Santa Ana): 'Tifway', 'Tifway II', 'Tifgreen'

Kansas: 'Tifway', 'Tifway II', 'Tifgreen'

Maryland: 'Tifgreen', 'Texturf 10', 'Tifway II'

Mississippi: 'Tifgreen', 'Tifway', 'Texturf 10'

New Mexico: 'Tifway II', 'Midiron', 'Tifgreen'

Virginia (Blacksburg): 'Vamont', 'Tifway', 'Tifway II'

Virginia (Virginia Beach): 'Tifway II', 'Tifway', 'Tufcote'

'**Tifway**' is the best all-purpose hybrid for bermudagrass lawns. It is aggressive, disease-resistant, and dark green. Although wear-tolerant, 'Tifway' makes a high-quality lawn only with a fair amount of care.

'**Tiflawn**' is not as fine-textured as 'Tifway', but it shares that variety's wear tolerance and disease resistance. It is also moderately cold-tolerant and drought-resistant.

'**Tifgreen**' and '**Tifdwarf**' are very fine-leaved varieties, used primarily for golf greens. They are not recommended for home lawns.

BAHIAGRASS

Bahiagrass is a coarse-textured, low growing perennial that spreads by means of short, thick rhizomes. Although it spreads slowly, it is very aggressive, and forms a thick turf that resists thatch.

But even named varieties like 'Paraguay' and 'Pensacola' do not make fine lawns. They produce a dense, rather uneven and coarse turf that is difficult to cut with a reel mower. The grass blades are so tough and strong that a sharp mower blade is required for a clean cut. The grass should be clipped at 2 inches. It is a fairly light feeder, requiring 2 to 4 pounds of nitrogen per 1,000 square feet, divided between spring and fall feedings. It has some drought tolerance, and grows best in the southern coastal plains.

Bahiagrass is the most shade-tolerant of all warm season grasses. Because it is very slow to germinate, a high seed rate (up to 10 pounds per 1,000 square feet) is required for quick cover. Spring planting

Seed head

Leaf sheath
and blade junction

Seed

Bahiagrass is too coarse-textured and uneven to make a good-looking turf.

'**Argentine**' is less coarse and is softer than common bahia, so it is more easily mowed. It is well adapted to southern Florida.

'**Paraguay**' is often grown in Texas. It is similar to 'Argentine', but 'Paraguay' is a heavy producer of seed heads and is very slow to germinate. It produces hairy blades with a dull sheen.

'**Paraguyan 22**' is coarser than 'Paraguay'.

'**Pensacola**' has the best germination rate of the species. This hardy, cold-tolerant variety has fine, glossy leaves.

'**Tifhi**' is a 'Pensacola' hybrid that is denser and leafier than other bahiagrasses.

'**Wilmington**' is fine-textured and dark green. Though similar to 'Pensacola', it is more cold-tolerant and is vegetatively propagated.

Seaside paspalum is a very fine-textured bahiagrass. It is tolerant of both salt and drought and is vegetatively propagated.

MORE SOUTHERN STANDOUTS

Blue gramagrass is a medium-fine, low-growing, bunch-type grass that forms a dense sod. It is adapted to the Great Plains and is well suited to alkali soils. Although it is drought-resistant, blue gramagrass becomes dormant and turns brown during severe drought. It is best used for turf in cool, dry areas. Blue

gives best results, although seed sown in the fall will overwinter and sprout in the spring. Seed at a rate of 2 to 3 pounds per 1,000 square feet in the spring. If mixed with fine fescue in the fall, this grass provides quick cover.

Common bahia winter-kills below 20°F. It is very coarse and is not recommended for turf.

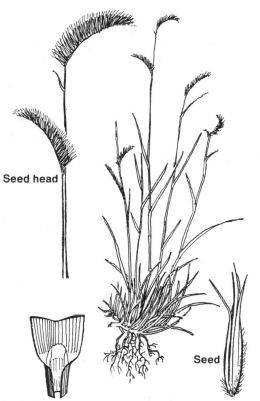

Seed head

Leaf sheath and blade junction

Seed

Blue gramagrass is a medium-fine, low-growing bunch grass that forms a dense sod.

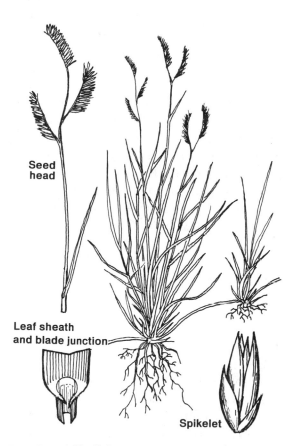

Seed head

Leaf sheath and blade junction

Spikelet

Fine-leaved buffalograss spreads by stolons to form a thick, drought-resistant sod.

gramagrass can be easily established in spring from seed planted at 1 to 1½ pounds per 1,000 square feet.

Buffalograss is one of the few native American grasses now used for turf. It is a fine-leaved, sod-forming perennial that spreads by stolons, and one of the best lawn grasses for the sunny sites and heavy clays of the Great Plains. Because it is very drought-resistant and tolerant of alkali conditions, buffalograss is catching on as a low-maintenance alternative to bermuda-grass in the West. In a given location, it requires less mowing and less nitrogen fertilizer than bermudagrass and is less invasive. Though drought-tolerant, buffalo-grass turns brown in midsummer and again when growth stops in the fall. Seed is expensive, usually well over $10 per pound. To establish a lawn of it, you need 7 pounds per 1,000 square feet.

Buffalograss can be started in spring from sod or hulled seed sown at a depth of no more than ¼ inch. There are no named varieties of buffalograss.

Carpetgrass is a coarse, low-growing, sod-forming perennial that spreads rapidly by stolons. It produces a dense, compact turf under low mowing. The grass resists disease and insect damage and can stand heavy traffic, and it will thrive with little fertilization in poor soils. Because carpetgrass grows well on sandy soils but is not drought-resistant, it is a good lawn grass for the lower coastal plain of the United States.

But carpetgrass is not for everyone. It does not tolerate salt spray, and will not grow well in regions that remain dry dur-ing part of the growing season. It is sensitive to a lack of iron, and must have a somewhat acidic soil if it is to pick up sufficient amounts of this nutrient. Carpet-grass should be mowed at 1 inch to prevent the formation of ugly seed heads. It is very cold-sensitive and winter-kills north of Augusta, Georgia. Even in the Deep South, it will turn brown over winter.

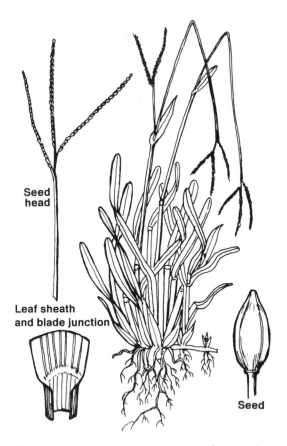

Seed head

Leaf sheath and blade junction

Seed

Carpetgrass is a coarse, low-growing, sod-forming perennial that spreads rapidly by stolons.

Carpetgrass can be established quickly by seeding, sprigging, or sodding. Seeding is the least expensive method. Sow in the spring at the rate of 3 or 4 pounds per 1,000 square feet. Sprigging (setting out small grass plants as explained in Chapter 3) and sodding may be done in late spring or early summer. There are no improved varieties.

Centipedegrass is a medium-coarse, sod-forming perennial that spreads rapidly by the creeping stolons that give the grass its name. Centipedegrass makes the best low-maintenance lawn in the Deep South as far north as North Carolina and northern Alabama. It can survive in the upper South, but will be discolored by frost. This grass grows on poor soils, maturing at a height of only 3 to 4 inches, and it requires less mowing than bermudagrass. You should have to get out the lawnmower only every 10 to 20 days.

Centipedegrass forms a dense, vigorous turf that is resistant to weed invasion. It requires less watering and fertilizing than other southern lawn grasses, is seldom damaged by disease, and is more tolerant of shade than bermudagrass. In fact, the main cause of trouble with centipedegrass is overfertilization. A single dose of nitrogen in the spring is all the food this grass needs. However, centipedegrass may develop yellow foliage from lack of iron, especially in alkaline soils. Given a good nutrient balance, it thrives on soils with a pH above 7. Iron sulfate or iron chelate can be used to green up the grass.

Centipedegrass may be seeded, sprigged,

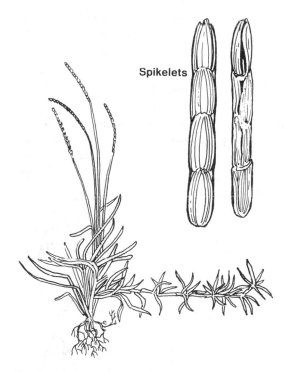

Spikelets

Centipedegrass is a medium-coarse, creeping grass that makes a good low-maintenance lawn in the Deep South.

or sodded. Seed is quite expensive by weight, up to $15 per pound, but because the seed is so small (500,000 per pound) it goes a long way. Rates of seeding vary from 3 ounces to 1 pound per 1,000 square feet. Sod should be planted in late spring or early summer. There are no improved varieties of seeded centipede, but 'Oaklawn' and 'Tennessee Hardy' can be vegetatively propagated.

St. Augustinegrass is a coarse-textured, sod-forming perennial that spreads by both stolons and rhizomes. Its main claim to fame is as a shade grass in the mid-South. Under the right conditions it forms a thick, dense turf that crowds out all other grasses and weeds. But St. Augustinegrass is by no means a low-maintenance turf. It grows best on soils that are fertile, well drained, and rich in organic matter, with a pH of 6 to 7. The grass requires abundant moisture, spring and fall feedings with a complete fertilizer, and a summer application of nitrogen. It is easily damaged by chinch bugs, leaf spot, and brown patch. It cries out for chemical maintenance. However, the new variety 'Floratam' is resistant to chinch bugs.

St. Augustine tends to build up a springy thatch that slows water penetration and encourages disease; as a result, it requires frequent vertical cutting with special equipment. In the mildest areas, it stays green throughout the winter. St. Augustine-grass is established from sprigging or sodding. It does not set viable seed.

Common St. Augustine and the variety *'Roselawn'* are both coarse and open, with few leafy branches and long internodes.

'Better Blue' is relatively dense and low growing. It is dark green, and well adapted to coastal environments.

'Floratine' is dense, less coarse, and tolerates close mowing.

THE PROS AND CONS OF ZOYSIA

Zoysias are coarse to fine (depending on the species), low-growing perennials that spread by stolons and rhizomes. They are often heralded as miracle grasses for most of the country. In truth they are something less than that, although they do make fine,

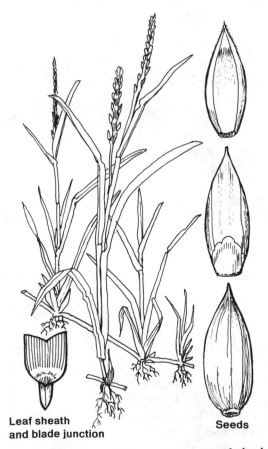

**Leaf sheath
and blade junction**

Seeds

St. Augustinegrass is a coarse-textured shade grass for the mid-South. However, it is quite susceptible to insect and disease damage.

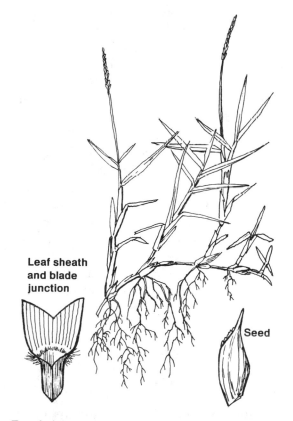

Leaf sheath and blade junction

Seed

Zoysia has coarse to fine blades (depending on the species) that make a good, wear-tolerant turf in the South.

that, while neighbors' lawns stay green until covered by snow, their own lawns begin to turn off-color in cold weather, becoming completely brown after the first frost. And in the spring, zoysia is slow to green up, not taking on color until warm weather is well under way.

In the transition zone, zoysias are often substituted for cool-season grasses, which are no match for crabgrass or other warm-season grasses. It's true that zoysia will keep out crabgrass, but its brown color in fall, winter, and spring is not much more attractive than the brown of crabgrass.

To their credit, zoysias are wear-resistant. They form a dense sod that chokes out weeds (and other grasses), but establish very slowly from sprigging, taking as long as two to three years to fill in. They have some drought tolerance, but because they are shallow-rooted they must be irrigated in dry areas. Zoysias tend to develop thatch over time, so they require some maintenance. Because they grow slowly, they do not need mowing as often as bermudagrass. Zoysias are light feeders, requiring only a single application of a complete fertilizer with 2 to 3 pounds of nitrogen per 1,000 square feet.

Of the three species, **Zoysia japonica** (also called Japanese or Korean lawn grass) is the most coarse, vigorous, and winter-hardy. Japonica prefers heavy soils, and requires fertilization for good growth and color. It is the only zoysia species that may be established from seed, but named varieties such as '**Meyer**' may not come true from seed. Sow at a rate of 1 to 2 pounds of

low-maintenance lawns in certain areas. Climatic adaptation and qualities vary among the three species.

All three species are warm-season grasses. And yet zoysias are sometimes sold in such cool states as New Jersey and Pennsylvania. There, homeowners will find

hulled seed per 1,000 square feet. For quick coverage, sprigs should be planted every 2 inches in rows 6 inches apart. 'Meyer' is a dense and hardy selection of this type.

Zoysia matrella (Manila grass) is intermediate in texture and winter-hardiness. It forms a dense, carpetlike turf that resists weeds, wear, disease, and insect damage. It also tolerates considerable shade, but liberal applications of nitrogen fertilizer are needed to produce fine, dark green leaves. **'Flawn'** is a variety that is hardy along the Mid-Atlantic states and is well adapted to the Southwest. **'Midwestern'** was developed for colder climates at Purdue University in Indiana.

Zoysia tenuifolia (mascarene grass) is the finest-textured and least winter-hardy zoysia. It is adapted to very few places in the country, though it grows with some success in southern California. It shares Manila grass's need for moisture, nutrients, and rich soil, but it is even less winter-hardy. It becomes sod-bound and humps as it becomes older, encouraging weed invasions.

'Emerald' is a hybrid between Japanese lawn grass and mascarene grass that has proven superior to 'Meyer' zoysia in the southern United States. This grass is fine-leaved, dense-growing, and dark green.

DICHONDRA, THE GRASS THAT ISN'T

Dichondra is a grass in function rather than in form. It can more accurately be called a groundcover that serves as a grass. This dicotyledon of the morning-glory family (Convolvulaceae) is used in the warmest regions of the country if soil is moist and fertility is low. Although it is an aggressive grass that may become a weed, its pale green, kidney-shaped leaves are rather delicate and do not stand traffic well.

Dichondra is not a low-maintenance alternative. It requires plenty of nitrogen, up to 1 pound per 1,000 square feet for every month of the growing season. It is subject to alternaria disease and is attractive to cutworms, flea beetles, slugs, and snails. It looks best when mowed to 1 inch.

Dichondra may be started from sprigs or seeded at the rate of 1 pound per 1,000 square feet. There are no named cultivars.

SAY NO TO THESE GRASSES

Broomsedge is a coarse-textured perennial bunch grass that is a common weed from the eastern United States to Texas.

Dallisgrass is a coarse-textured perennial bunch grass, and an objectionable weed in turfgrass.

Kikuyugrass is a coarse-textured, sod-forming perennial that spreads by rhizomes and stolons. Although adapted to higher elevations, it is not recommended for turf.

MADE FOR THE SHADE

Shade is one of the most common problems facing the lawn owner. About one-fifth of the lawn area in the United States is growing in some sort of shade, and most of that grass is probably struggling for survival. Shady areas tend to be patchy and weak, invaded by weeds, and infected by diseases. But it doesn't have to be that way. Many grasses will hold their own in up to 70 percent shade. Even some formerly shade-shy species will grow well without full sun, thanks to new and improved varieties.

If you look for shade-loving species in most books, you'll find fine fescues, zoysias, St. Augustinegrass, and bentgrass at the top of the list, with tall fescue, Kentucky bluegrass, and perennial ryegrass near the bottom. But improved varieties of the latter three outperform the standard of their species and even take to the shade better than some of the more shade-tolerant species. In a trial of four tall fescue varieties — 'Alta', 'Falcon', 'Rebel', and 'Houndog' — all cultivars made an acceptable stand under 70 percent tree shade. Among the Kentucky bluegrasses, 'Glade', 'Nugget', 'Bristol', and 'Benson' show the best shade tolerance.

Out-of-date lawn literature advises against planting perennial ryegrass in the shade, because perennial ryegrass was not known for its ability to grow in the shade until the improved varieties hit the market. 'Prelude' and 'Repell' both grow well in moderate shade. Still, perennial ryegrass shouldn't be your first choice in heavy shade (see the box at left, How They Handle the Shade, for better choices).

SHADE STRATEGIES

If you have a shady yard, you aren't necessarily stuck with a poor lawn. You can both lessen the shade and increase your lawn's chances of surviving it.

Shade does more than reduce the amount of light available for photosynthesis. It can encourage disease, because grass stays wet and the air is usually stagnant, and these conditions favor most disease fungi, especially powdery mildew.

HOW THEY HANDLE THE SHADE

A four-year trial at Rutgers University in New Jersey shows how variety effects shade tolerance. The varieties are listed in order of their performance under heavy shade.

'Rebel' tall fescue

'A-34' Kentucky bluegrass

'Reliant' hard fescue

'Scaldis' hard fescue

'Jamestown' Chewings fescue

'Biljart' hard fescue

'Banner' Chewings fescue

'Kentucky 31' tall fescue

'Pennfine' perennial ryegrass

'Fortress' red fescue

'Nugget' Kentucky bluegrass

'Highlight' Chewings fescue

'Ruby' red fescue

'Park' Kentucky bluegrass

'Glade' Kentucky bluegrass

'Linn' perennial ryegrass

Start by sowing disease-resistant varieties. Increase air flow through the area by trimming shrubs. Reduce the shade by pruning lower tree branches and thinning higher ones to open up the middle of the tree.

To survive in the shade, grasses need extra pampering. Because photosynthesis is reduced, grass in shade needs all the surface area it can get, so mow ½ to 1 inch higher than normal.

If grass is trying to grow under a tree, it also faces competition from the tree for moisture and nutrients. As a rule of thumb, increase the fertilizer dose by half. Shaded lawns may need regular deep watering, but take care not to leave standing water on the blades.

SHOPPING FOR SEED

When buying grass seed, you get what you pay for. Fortunately, every package of grass seed has a label, which is required to contain certain information. It must list the amount of five things that might be in that bag or box.

First, there's the turfgrass, which is listed in percentage. There may be one or more species with several varieties of each. They must be listed as either fine- or coarse-textured.

The next three are grouped in a general category of "other ingredients." That may include weed seed, inert matter, and crop seeds, also listed in percentage.

Finally, noxious weeds, as determined by your state agriculture department, will be listed separately, not by percentage but by numbers per pound.

Let's take a closer look at each of these elements, starting with the worst first. Noxious weeds are plants defined by state law as being particularly harmful. They may include such villains as wild garlic, buckhorn plantain, and annual bluegrass. In some states, it's illegal to sell mixes that contain certain noxious weeds like quack grass. Top-quality seed will contain no noxious weeds.

The ingredient called "crop seed" may be even more troublesome in turf mixes. It includes seeds of plants that may be perfectly harmless under other conditions, such as timothy, rough bluegrass, orchardgrass, and bentgrass. They're normally not considered weeds, unless they show up in a lawn where they don't belong. Just 1 percent of a contaminant grass can produce 40 plants per square foot. That's enough to ruin the looks of a lawn. A good mix should contain well below 1 percent of crop seeds.

Inert matter includes chaff, hulls, stones, and such. It won't harm the mixture, but you don't want to be paying for more than 3 percent.

Weed seed includes common weeds, not classified as noxious. There should be none.

Now, to the turfgrasses. They are listed in descending order by the percent present in the mixture (also called purity) and the germination percentage of each. Combine those two numbers and you get a figure not too many lawn owners know about: real value. Though it's not on the label, the real value is a good measure of the quality of the seed. To determine the figure, multiply the percentage of the contents by the germination percent and divide by 100. Suppose you buy a box of 'Merion' Kentucky bluegrass. If it's listed as 90 percent pure with an 80 percent germination rate, multiply 90 by 80 and divide by 100. The real value is 72 percent. This means that 72 percent of what's in the box will produce 'Merion' Kentucky bluegrass. The other 28 percent will be something else. You can use these numbers to compare the value of different brands. For example, a 95-percent-pure seed with an 80 percent germination rate is a better value than an 80-percent-pure, 90-percent-germination seed. To figure the real value of a mix (different species) or a blend (different varieties of the same species), compute the real value of each grass, then add them together.

There are industry standards that regulate the minimum purity and germination percentages allowable for all species. To be sold legally, Kentucky bluegrass, for example, must be at least 90 percent pure and have a germination rate of at least 75 percent.

Check the type of grasses in the mixture. For most lawn uses, you'll want only fine-textured grass. Stay away from mixes that contain coarse kinds.

Finally, look for variety names. Where available, choose only improved, named varieties. Stay away from mixes that list just Kentucky bluegrass or common Kentucky bluegrass. Instead, choose something like 'Merion' Kentucky bluegrass. Make sure the box does not contain annual ryegrass or other annual grasses. Finally, when shopping, remember your yard's conditions (shade, drought, and so on), and bear in mind which grass varieties meet those conditions.

To get you started, here are just a few recommended mixes and blends for some typical conditions.

■ A good general-purpose turfgrass for cool-region lawns is a mix of named Kentucky bluegrass and red fescue.

■ For shade, a mix should include more fescue than bluegrass. Another option is a 40-40-20 mix of named Kentucky bluegrass, red fescue, and perennial ryegrass. For heavy use, plant 95 percent named turf type tall fescue with 5 percent Kentucky bluegrass.

■ For open, sunny locations, a good mix is 40 to 60 percent 'Merion' Kentucky bluegrass, with the remainder made up of other improved bluegrasses.

■ An equal mix of improved red fescue and improved Kentucky bluegrass is also good for the sun.

COPING WITH IMPOSSIBLE SITES

Even the new, improved turfgrasses will not thrive in every situation. Sometimes it's just a waste of effort to try to grow a lawn. If you have an area that's too shady, rocky, sandy, or steep for grass, that's the place to plant a groundcover. They're also good for spots that you just don't want to mow.

Groundcovers are perennial plants that creep, crawl, sprawl, or bunch to cover the soil. Most don't need mowing; few can stand wear and tear. They're meant for looking at, not walking on. There are two primary types of groundcovers: herbaceous perennials and woody plants.

THE BEST HERBACEOUS GROUNDCOVERS

Most herbaceous perennials die back to the ground in the winter, but they return with renewed vigor in the spring. They spread rapidly, and most will fill in an area in the first season.

Airplane plant (*Chlorophytum comosum* and *C. elatum*) is a tropical lilylike plant that grows to 8 inches tall. It spreads rapidly and will fill in well when planted on 1-foot spacings. These shade-loving plants will not survive frost. However, they are drought-resistant.

Crown vetch (*Coronilla varia*) is one of the best groundcovers for banks, and is frequently used to stabilize soil along highways. This sprawling perennial creeper is a member of the pea family. It features finely cut, light green leaves and lovely pink to white flower clusters in the summer.

Japanese snakebeard (*Ophiopogon japonica*) is a small lily with grasslike leaves, growing 8 to 12 inches high with purple or white berries. It can be planted in either sun or shade, and thrives in poor soils. Because it is slow-spreading, it must be planted 3 to 6 inches apart for good cover. Japanese snakebeard is hardy as far north as New York State.

Lamb's-ear (*Stachys olympica*) has large, gray, semi-evergreen leaves that cover the ground like a mat. It thrives in any soil and is very hardy.

Lily-of-the-valley (*Convallaria majalis*) grows rapidly to form a dense mat in full to partial shade. Tiny, white, bell-like flowers bloom in May on the hardy, 6-inch-tall plants.

Lippia (*Lippia canescens*) is a frost-tender creeper with dark leaves. It grows only 1 inch tall and can be mowed to form a dense sod.

Peppermint (*Mentha piperita*) is a vigorous creeper that grows up to 2 feet high. It is invasive, and should be clipped back to the ground every few years to keep it neat. The dull green leaves make a fragrant, invigorating tea.

Silver mound (*Artemisia schmidtiana* 'Nana') has fine-leaved, silvery foliage. Plants grow to 8 inches high, and spread 12 inches. Silver mound prefers hot, dry conditions.

Trailing spiderwort (*Tradescantia zebrina*) is the familiar wandering jew, most often grown as an indoor hanging plant. But in frost-free areas, it can serve as a vigorous groundcover. The variegated purple-and-green leaves will completely cover an area in a season when the plants are spaced 4 to 6 inches apart.

PROVEN WOODY GROUNDCOVERS

Woody plants may be vining or shrublike. Some are deciduous, others are evergreen. They are long-lasting, but normally are slower to fill in than herbaceous perennials. All of the woody plants in the following list are evergreens except bugle.

Aaron's beard (*Hypericum calycinum*) is a shrub that grows 1 foot tall. Hardy to

USDA Hardiness Zone 4, it does best in shady areas with sandy, well-drained soil.

Bugle (*Ajuga genevensis*) may be grown in full sun or partial shade. This creeping mint relative bears 6-inch-tall flower stalks in spring. The leaves are light green and puckered. It is hardy throughout the country.

Creeping juniper (*Juniperus horizontalis*) is one of the few conifers used as a groundcover. There are several varieties, ranging in height from a few inches to over a foot. The scaly, evergreen leaves may be bluish-green, steel blue, or yellow. Creeping juniper is at its best in the northern states and may be grown south to about the latitude of New Jersey. It spreads rapidly in rocky or sandy soil but will not tolerate drought.

Ivies (*Hedera* spp.) are evergreen vines that grow in dense shade and full sun. They're recommended for steep banks, bare spaces around trees, or areas where they can climb to cover rocks. There are species that thrive in every climate of the United States with all manner and color of leaves. They spread rapidly; when planted 6 to 12 inches apart, they will cover an area in one season.

Japanese honeysuckle (*Lonicera japonica*) is such a quick-covering plant that it has become a pest in many parts of the country, especially the Northeast. It is a climbing or sprawling vine with fragrant yellow, pink, red, or white blossoms. The small oval leaves are semi-evergreen, and may remain on the vine until midwinter in the North. It is best used on steep banks and where it cannot invade other plantings.

Japanese spurge (*Pachysandra terminalis*) is one of the best evergreen groundcovers in areas between the cooler portions of the Gulf Coast States and southern New England. It will grow in sun or shade in the North, but needs shade and plenty of water to survive in the South. This low-growing plant spreads by underground suckers and has attractive, glossy, dark green leaves. It grows in ordinary soil, and makes a dense cover under trees where grass will not grow. Cuttings should be spaced 4 to 6 inches apart for good cover.

Moss pink (*Phlox subulata*) is a good groundcover for rocky soils. The 6-inch-tall creeping plant produces mounds of pink, purple, or white flowers in spring.

Mother-of-thyme (*Thymus serpyllum*) is a very low, creeping evergreen, often planted between stones or bricks in a walk. It thrives in hot, dry, rocky soil in full sun. Flowers may be white, lavender, crimson, or purple, and the leaves are fragrant.

Partridgeberry (*Mitchella repens*) is a diminutive evergreen with small round or oval glossy leaves and a compact growth habit. It will grow well in either shade or moist sunny spots, and bears pairs of fragrant, pinkish-white flowers in spring. The flowers are followed by bright red berries in fall and winter.

Periwinkle (*Vinca minor*) is a hardy, low-growing perennial that spreads by creeping stems. It has small, dark green, glossy leaves with blue-violet flowers in spring. Periwinkle will form a dense mat that shades out weeds and grasses when grown in moist, shady sites. Spaced 4 to 8 inches apart, the plants will cover the ground in one or two seasons.

Scotch heather (*Calluna vulgaris*) offers many different flower and leaf colors on plants 4 to 24 inches tall. This clumping plant likes acid, moist soil in sun or shade.

Spring heath (*Erica carnea*) has needle-like leaves ranging in color from blue to yellow to bright green, and rosy red flowers. Plants grow from 6 to 12 inches tall in sun or shade.

Stonecrops (*Sedum* spp.) are succulent evergreens that thrive in dry soil. They are excellent on stony sites, slopes, or banks. Stonecrops have small, fleshy leaves and a wide variety of flower colors.

Wintercreeper (*Euonymus fortunei*) is a climbing evergreen, hardy except in the coldest parts of the country. Its small leaves turn purple in autumn and winter. It will grow in almost any soil and exposure.

Wintergreen (*Gaultheria procumbens*) is native to the eastern United States, and needs an acid, moist soil. It grows to 4 inches high. The foliage and fruit are very fragrant when crushed. Wintergreen grows best in shade.

Although most groundcovers are tough customers, they all can benefit from good soil. If possible, the ground should be dug deeply, to at least a foot, while working in a 2-inch layer of manure or compost. It's best to plant groundcovers in spring or fall, or when moisture is plentiful and temperatures are below 80°F. They should be planted in an equidistant pattern, 3 to 12 inches apart depending on how rapidly they spread.

3

SEEDING, SODDING, AND SPRIGGING

The new miracle turfgrasses can make any lawn better. And a yard planted with them makes your work easier. But they will never live up to their potential unless your timing is right.

No matter how disease-resistant, drought-tolerant, or otherwise miraculous the seed may be, it won't do you any good unless it germinates quickly and thickly. You can always mulch and water and nurse seedlings along, but you'll save a lot of labor if you sow at the right time of year.

Otherwise you'll be fighting a losing battle against weeds, drought, heat, and eventually insects and disease.

The idea is to sow the seed when weather conditions favor quick growth of grass and slow germination of weed seeds. This makes it harder for the weeds to get a foothold. But if the weather is too hot, too cold, or too dry for fast and uniform germination, the grass stand will leave bare spots. And those trouble spots are patches of weeds waiting to happen.

WHEN TO SOW?

What is the best time of year to sow grass? That depends on where your lawn is. It's determined by your geographical area, your climate, and the type of grass you choose.

The country is divided into five grass growing zones (explained on pages 17 and 18 of Chapter 2). In zones one (the North), three (the Plains), and five (the Northwest), you'll be planting cool-season grasses. First, consider what conditions they need for germination. Cool-season grasses germinate best at soil temperatures of 60° to 80°F. Those conditions most often occur in spring and fall. But there's more to it than temperature at sowing time. You have to consider the weather conditions both then and in the weeks to follow.

Moisture is the second key element. Though April showers will benefit young seedlings, a drought may be right around the corner. Cool-season grass sown in the spring has to face the stresses of summer all too soon. Young roots can't deal with drought because they're just not long enough to forage deeply for water.

Consider the competition grass will face from weeds. In most areas of the country, annual weed seeds are most viable in spring. They're programmed to sprout at that time of year, rather than in the fall, and they present serious competition to grass seedlings. If the weeds get a jump and come up first, the grass is at a disadvantage and so are you. Getting weeds out of a lawn is no easy task. It makes more sense to prevent them from gaining a foothold. When grass germinates quickly, it takes over and doesn't allow weeds any elbow room.

In the North, annual weeds are finishing their life cycles in the fall, so it's best to sow a lawn when the summer heat breaks around late August or September. Weed seeds are not geared to germinate then, but the grass seeds will succeed if they miss summer heat and drought. A young lawn can easily handle cool fall weather as long as the plants are six to eight weeks old before the first hard frost. If you do sow in spring, do so as soon as the ground can be worked—in general, no later than mid-May.

It's a different story in the South. Fall is a poor time for sowing grass there, because southern weeds operate on a different schedule. Many of them germinate in the fall, and grasses sown then have to face the competition from such winter annual weeds as chickweed, henbit, field pansy, and speedwell. The best time to sow a southern lawn is spring and early summer, from March until June when soil temperatures range between 70° to 95°F. A new lawn may need watering daily until it's established, but it will be able to handle hot weather better than the weeds it would face if planted in late summer. If you're in the transition zone between northern zone one and southern zone two, the best time for sowing depends on the type of grass: fall for cool-season, spring for warm-season. The only exception is when overseeding a warm-season grass with a cool-season grass, as you will see in the section on overseeding, pages 61 and 62.

But what if you move into a new house when it's not the ideal sowing time? You aren't likely to want to put up with living in the middle of a sandbox for two or three months. You *can* start a lawn nearly anytime, even in the heat of summer or dead of winter, but you'll be throwing good seed away. It makes more sense to plant an interim lawn to fill in until the time is right to plant your permanent grass.

In the North, annual ryegrass makes a good temporary lawn. It germinates quickly, grows quickly, and covers a lot of ground. Ryegrass will die off over the winter, but by then its job will have been done. You can either till under the ryegrass in the fall and plant a permanent lawn in its place, or let it winter-kill, rake out the dead grass, and overseed with a permanent seed mix early in the spring. This may seem like a lot of work, but it will be worth the effort. The next-best method would be to add ½ pound of annual ryegrass to your permanent lawn mix when you seed. The ryegrass will fill in quickly, and after it dies the permanent grass will spread and take over.

In the South, you can sow warm-season grasses from April to August. At any other time, start a cool-season nurse crop. Follow the same procedure as for northern lawns, above, but use perennial ryegrass instead. Then overseed or reseed in the spring.

The nurse crop of ryegrass will germinate quickly in any region. It will cover the ground and keep weeds from taking over. If you till it in before planting a new lawn, you get a second benefit—the rye acts as a green manure, adding organic matter to improve the soil.

SOIL PREP

You almost certainly have to take the time to prepare the soil for a new lawn. You may need to test and improve the soil, and to correct drainage or grading problems. Whether you're starting from scratch at a new site or renovating or reseeding your old lawn, you've probably got some work ahead of you.

If your house is new, the topsoil may have been laid waste and compacted by the contractors. Or if your lawn is old and shabby, there's probably a reason it needs fixing, and most likely that reason is the soil. Sowing more seed into that bad soil is like painting over rotten wood. It's not worth the effort. So spend some time analyzing and correcting the problem.

MAKING THE GRADE

First, take a look at the grading of your yard. Ideally, a lawn should slope 3 to 6 degrees away from your house—that's equal to a 1-foot drop for every running 100 feet. To measure the grade, sink a 3-foot stake 1 foot into the ground as near to your house as possible. Then measure off 100 feet. You don't have to be precise, and pacing will do. (Depending on your stride, 30 to 40 paces should equal 100 feet.) At that point, sink another 3-foot post 1 foot into the ground.

Tie a light but sturdy string to the first stake at ground level. Stretch it taut to the other stake, and have a helper fasten a line level (available from a hardware store) to the midpoint of the string. Raise or lower the string until it's level, then tie it to the second stake. The distance between that point on the stake and the ground is the rate of drop per 100 feet. If the rate is less than 6 inches or more than 2½ feet in any direction, and you have had problems with water sitting in puddles or eroding the soil, you should consider re-grading. The job involves moving a lot of soil, and you'll probably want to call in a contractor. Just make sure he scrapes off the topsoil first and piles it out of the way

so that it can be replaced after the grading is done.

If the ground is too steep to grade gradually throughout, consider building terraces or berms. If the overall grade of your lawn falls within the guidelines, but there are bumps, hills, or low spots here and there, you can grade them out with a shovel, rake, wheelbarrow, and elbow grease.

Getting the proper slope is a good start, but it doesn't ensure that your drainage problems will be solved. If the grade of your soil is adequate but the water does not drain away two or three hours after a good rain or watering, you may have to install drainage pipes. These 4-inch plastic pipes can be purchased at any home center. Before you buy them, lay out a drainage pattern on the lawn. First, you should fig-

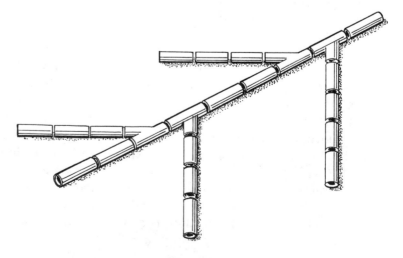

Ideally, drainage tile should be laid out in lateral lines, 20 feet apart and branching out in a herringbone pattern.

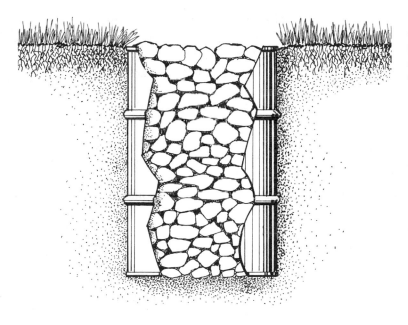

A good dry well can be made from a 55-gallon drum with both ends removed. Sink the drum below hardpan, and fill it with stones.

ure out what they are going to drain to. It could be a storm sewer, a street gutter or roadside ditch, a stream or pond on your property, or a dry well that you'll dig at the lowest point on your property.

The illustration on page 56 shows a drainage system with lateral branch lines emptying into a mainline. These branches are roughly 20 feet apart, and placed in a herringbone pattern. The drain pipes should be 4 to 6 inches below the soil surface and pitched at a grade of 3 to 6 inches per 100 feet. Cut the pipes as necessary, lay them in trenches lined with gravel or porous landscape fabric, fasten them together, seal the joints with epoxy, and cover with topsoil.

Water the area thoroughly after installation to help the soil settle. After a week or so, fill in depressions (if necessary) before seeding the lawn.

A dry well can be constructed of brick, cinder block, or stone, but the easiest way is to use an empty 55-gallon drum with both ends cut off. Locate the low spot where you want the drainage tile to empty and start digging. You'll need a pit wide enough to hold the drum and deep enough so that the top of the drum will be below the lowest point of the drainage pipe. For the dry well to work, the bottom will have to be positioned *below* any hardpan or rock. Lower the drum into the pit, fill it with gravel and small stones, and position the tile so that it drains into the drum. Surround the drum with more gravel and stones, cover it with sand and a light layer of topsoil, then seed over the top.

GETTING THE SOIL IN SHAPE

If your soil is heavy clay, many of your drainage problems can be solved by improving the texture of the soil. Sandy soils may have a different kind of drainage problem—water runs through them too fast. Either way, you can fix the texture with organic matter. In fact, any kind of soil can be improved with the addition of organic matter.

Start by analyzing the texture and content of your soil as explained in Chapter 1. If your soil is more than 60 percent clay or 70 percent sand, work in at least a 2-inch layer of organic matter or a 3-inch layer of rich topsoil. The organic matter can be compost, peat moss, dried manure, rice hulls, or any combination of the above. Before adding the organic matter, have your soil tested for fertility and add appropriate amounts of nitrogen, phosphorus, or potash. Use bloodmeal, cottonseed meal, or leather dust to provide nitrogen. Rock phosphate and bonemeal will supply phosphorus. Greensand and wood ashes provide potash. Unless you have the soil test done by a lab that specializes in organic recommendations, such as LaRamie Soils Service (P.O. Box 255, Laramie, WY 82070) or Woods End Laboratory (RFD Box 128, Temple, ME 04984), it will come back with instructions for adding chemical fertilizers. Use the information in Chapter 4 to convert them to amounts of organic fertilizer.

A good basic fertilizer for a newly seeded lawn includes 2 to 3 pounds of nitrogen, 5 to 8 pounds of phosphorus, and 2 to 3 pounds of potash per 1,000 square feet. An organic mix would provide that in 25 pounds each of bloodmeal, bonemeal, and greensand. Or you can use a commercial mix such as Erth-Rite. Sprinkle the additives over the layer of organic matter, then till or disc to a depth of 6 inches. Add lime if necessary.

If you're starting with bare soil, you're now just about ready to sow. But to renovate an old lawn, you first have to get rid of the old sod, thatch, and weeds. You can rent a sod stripper to slice this top layer, or you can hire someone to do it for you. The problem with slicing is that you lose some valuable topsoil with the sod. Instead, you can plow under the old turf to bury all remnants of the sod and still leave the soil in good shape. But buried sod breaks down slowly, and can present a barrier against root and water penetration. A rotary tiller slices sod and mixes it with the soil rather than burying it, but a tiller will take several passes to do the job. And the soil still won't be ready for planting. You'll have to carefully rake out roots, stems, and thatch.

Instead of raking, you can delay planting to let the tilled-in sod decompose. That will take from one month, under hot conditions, to as long as a year, in cool areas. But you can speed the breakdown by working in a material high in nitrogen.

A rotary tiller can slice up old sod to prepare the lawn for replanting.

HOW TO SOW

Finally you're ready to buy the seed. Refer to the table, How Much Seed Do You Need? on page 60, to determine the amount you need. The information in Chapter 2 will help you decide which mixture is best for your conditions. After the soil has been prepared, rake it smooth. Grade out any dips or lumps and spread the seed.

Divide the correct amount of seed into two equal portions. Put half in the seeder or, if you're sowing by hand, in a bucket. Make one pass over the area with the first batch of seed. Use the rest of the seed to make a second pass perpendicular to the first.

Use a rake to cover the seed lightly with soil. Firm the seeded area by rolling lightly with a lawn roller, or by tamping with the back of a rake. Mulching with a light covering of weed-free straw will conserve moisture and prevent rain or watering from washing away the seed. One bale of straw weighing 60 to 80 pounds will mulch 1,000 square feet. Do not use hay—it contains weed seeds. Neither peat moss nor sawdust are suitable either, because they may crust over into an impenetrable layer. The new wide-spun polyester row covers are expensive, but they make an excellent mulch for newly seeded lawns. They shield the soil from wind and sun and keep in moisture. Use pins made from clothes hangers to keep the mulch in place. Remove row covers when the grass reaches 1 inch in height.

On terraced areas or sloping banks, you can use cheesecloth, burlap, or com-

Spread a thin layer of bloodmeal or a thicker layer of dried manure. Grass clippings are also high in nitrogen, and you can add them to help these amendments. Here's how. Before tilling in the sod, let the grass grow high, up to 5 or 6 inches. Then mow the grass as close as possible and remove all the clippings. Till in the sod, then spread the clippings over the area and till them in. Why not just till in the grass without cutting it first? Because simply tilling the sod won't kill it; clumps may regrow and resist breakdown.

HOW MUCH SEED DO YOU NEED?

Cool-Season Grasses	Seeding Rate (lb./1,000 sq. ft.)	Time to Emergence
Bentgrasses	½–1	Fast (7–12 days)
Kentucky bluegrass	1–2	Slow (20–28 days)
Chewings fescue	3–5	Medium (10–21 days)
Creeping fescue	3–5	Medium (10–21 days)
Meadow fescue	3–4	Fast (7–14 days)
Red fescue	3–4	Medium (10–21 days)
Tall fescue	5–8	Medium (10–21 days)
Redtop	1–2	Fast (8–10 days)
Common ryegrass	4–6	Fast (7–14 days)
Perennial ryegrass	4–8	Fast (7–14 days)

Warm-Season Grasses		
Bahiagrass	5	Fast
Bermudagrass	1–3	Fast
Blue gramagrass	1–1½	Slow
Buffalograss	5–7	Slow
Carpetgrass	3–4	Medium
Centipedegrass	¼–1	Medium

mercial mulching cloth to hold in moisture and keep seeds from washing away. Grass will grow through these mulching materials, which can be left to rot.

After the grass has been sown, water it with care until it is well established. You cannot allow the soil surface to dry out until the grass is 2 inches tall, even if it means watering once, twice, or even more often each day. The irrigation should be regular but light. Do not saturate the soil, or you will risk encouraging disease. When the grass first comes up, stay off the area, and do not mow until it is at least 2 or perhaps 3 inches tall.

Researchers at Pennsylvania State University found that the first mowing of a newly seeded lawn has a big effect on grass establishment, especially for a mixture of bluegrass and ryegrass. Ryegrass is much more vigorous than Kentucky bluegrass at an early age—it took perennial ryegrass only five weeks to cover 90 percent of the test plot with foliage, while bluegrass didn't cover that well until the next season. Consequently, a ryegrass and bluegrass mix can give you a much higher percentage of ryegrass than you bargained for, because its strong early growth forces out the bluegrass.

The researchers reasoned that mowing at the right time and height might swing the balance in favor of the bluegrass. They tried waiting from one to seven weeks after sowing until the first mowing, setting the mower at heights ranging from ½ to 1½ inches.

Normally, Kentucky bluegrass is first mowed seven weeks after sowing. But that gives ryegrass time to get up and shade the ground, slowing the growth of bluegrass. Instead, the researchers found that mowing the mixture just two weeks after sowing, at ½ inch, favored the bluegrass. The longer they waited to make that first mowing, the greater the percentage of ryegrass in the final mix. They recommend mowing at the close height for two weeks, then raising it to 1½ inches. By following this regimen with a 3-to-1 seed mix of ryegrass and bluegrass, they wound up with a 50/50 stand of the two grasses.

OVERSEEDING

You can have a new lawn without ripping up the old one by overseeding with a new grass. First, you have to decide if your lawn is worth overseeding. Use the method discussed in Chapter 1 to measure the percentage of good grass in your lawn. A lawn that is less than 50 percent good grass is not worth trying to save, and the easiest path, in the long run, would be to dig it up and start all over. But if there is more than 50 percent grass, you can repair it by overseeding.

Overseeding is a good choice if your whole lawn simply looks ragged, or if you want to switch over to one or more of the new low-maintenance grasses that offer resistance to pests and diseases. Or maybe you just don't like the looks of your grass. It might be a coarse species that compares unfavorably with your neighbors' lawns.

There are many ways to overseed, with increasing degrees of difficulty and corresponding rates of success. But whichever method you use, the best time to overseed cool-season grasses is fall, approximately six weeks before your first fall frost. Warm-season grasses can be overseeded in the spring.

If you're dealing with a small area—1,000 square feet or less—the only tools you need for overseeding are a good, heavy, metal garden rake and a lawnmower. First, mow the lawn closely, at half the normal mowing height and as low as ½ inch, depending on the species. Next, rake the lawn thoroughly. Use some muscle to remove all the clippings and as much thatch as possible, so that you expose a good deal of soil. Pull, cut, or hoe out any weeds. Rake the lawn one more time to rough up the soil and give the new seed a place to take root.

Now it's time to sow the seed. The seeding rate will vary from species to species. For overseeding, use 1½ times the amount recommended on the seed package. For example, perennial ryegrass calls for a rate of 4 to 6 pounds per 1,000 square feet; overseed it at 6 to 9 pounds. Use a drop spreader, or toss the seed by hand in wide arcs as you walk slowly over the area.

After sowing, go over the area once again with the garden rake, lightly this time. For best results, top-dress the area with a thin layer of sand or topsoil. You need only about ½ cubic yard (1½ cubic feet) per 1,000 square feet. Water the lawn well, putting down at least an inch of water. Then stay off the overseeded area until well after the grass comes up—two to four weeks.

While you're waiting for the grass to appear, keep it watered. Do not let the soil dry out at all. This is one time when it's all right, even beneficial, to water lightly every morning if necessary. Once the grass comes up, don't mow until it reaches its maximum mowing height (as noted in the table, Mowing Heights, on page 91.

For larger areas, it pays to rent a verticutter or slice seeder, available at tool rental shops. The verticutter is like a lawnmower with blades set on end. It slices through the thatch and soil, making a good environment for grass seed to germinate. Run the machine over the entire area in one direction, then run it over the lawn again in a perpendicular direction. Finally, sow as directed above. A slice seeder will cut the sod and sow the seed in one operation.

OVERSEEDING IN THE SOUTH

In the South, you can overseed a cool-season grass over summer grass in the fall to have winter color. Some people overseed annually to keep the lawn green year-round.

For best results, overseed a bermuda-grass lawn with bluegrass, perennial ryegrass, or annual ryegrass; results are not good over zoysia. In late August or September, clip the grass to 1 inch high or less. Rake the lawn thoroughly with a heavy metal rake. Then sow the overseeded grass at 1½ times the normal rate. Continue mowing at a height of 1 inch until the bermudagrass stops growing, usually by the end of October. Then raise the mower height to 2 inches, and mow when the grass reaches 3 inches. Continue to mow at this height through the winter. In summer, as the cool-season grass goes dormant, the warm-season grass will take over again.

SODDING

Laying sod may be a fast way to establish a lawn, but don't think it's any easier than seeding. The soil must be prepared just as carefully, and proper timing is just as important. Sod is much more expensive than seed, but it's especially good for establishing grass on slopes where seed would be washed away.

Shop for sod that is no more than 1 inch thick, otherwise it will have a hard time establishing. The ideal thickness is ¾ inch. Check the edges of the sod strips to make sure the soil has not been allowed to dry out. The grass should be uniformly green, with no brown patches, and clipped close.

The best time for sodding is the best time for seeding — fall in the North, spring in the South. Because sod is even more sensitive than seed to drought, do not attempt to lay sod during hot, dry weather.

Proceed as in the seeding instructions above. Correct drainage. Improve soil texture, and add amendments as necessary. Once the soil is ready, give it one last raking, and then firm the seedbed with a roller. Water gently until it is wet to a depth of 6 inches, without turning the top into mud.

Sodding shouldn't be rushed, and yet you shouldn't allow the sod to heat up as it sits in a pile. Don't have it delivered until the day you are ready to put it in place.

To start the first strips of sod, lay them against a straight edge — a 2-by-4, a line stretched between two stakes, or a sidewalk. Lay the sod strips as you would brick, fitting them together as tightly as possible but not overlapping. After laying the first strip, place a broad board on it for you to kneel on while working on the next strip. Make sure the edges of the second strip are in good contact with the first. At the same time, take care that you don't line up the patches exactly with the first. Instead, stagger the edges like a brick wall with a running bond configuration. In other words, place the strips so that their edges are

stepped across the lawn. Once the lawn is set down, firm the sod with a light roller.

When sodding a slope, use pegs or staples made from coat hangers to keep the sod from slipping down the hill. Don't push them in too far — they'll have to come out before you roll the sod. Replace the pegs or staples after the sod has been rolled, then remove them again after the sod is established.

After the sod has been rolled, top-dress it with a small amount of topsoil. Work the topdressing into the cracks between the sod pieces with a broom or the back of a wooden

Lay sod in a running bond pattern, so that the edges of the strips are staggered.

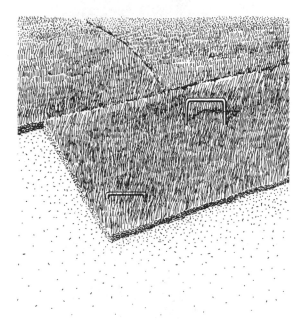

Staples made from coat hangers will keep sod in place on hills.

grow true to type. Instead, you'll have to use a vegetative means such as spot sodding, strip sodding, or sprigging.

Spot sodding is the process of planting small plugs or blocks of sod at intervals in the soil. Unlike regular sodding, bare patches are left in the soil for the grass to fill in. The plugs are usually 2-inch squares, and the blocks are 12-inch squares.

Prepare the ground as described above for sodding. But instead of laying the blocks on top of the soil, dig holes 2 to 3 inches deep and 1 foot apart. Then plant the plugs or blocks firmly into them. For quicker establishment, plant them closer. Strip sodding is similar, but strips 2 to 4 inches wide are planted in rows 1 foot apart.

Sprigging involves planting individual plants, runners, cuttings, or stolons at spaced intervals. These are made by tear-

rake. Keep the soil moist until the sod is well established. That means watering during the warmest part of each day until the roots have knitted themselves into the soil.

OTHER WAYS TO MAKE A LAWN

If you're planning on putting in a lawn of zoysia or one of the new improved varieties of bermudagrass, centipedegrass, creeping bentgrass, or velvet bentgrass, don't bother shopping for seed. It's not available, because seed of these varieties will not

Plugs are mini-strips of sod that are spaced and allowed to fill in.

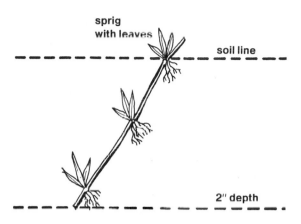

Sprigs are individual plants or runners of grass, usually planted 6 to 12 inches apart.

ing apart or shredding solid pieces of sod. The planting distance depends on grass species, and how fast you want to establish a lawn. Sprigs of Bermuda, centipede, and St. Augustinegrass are usually planted 12 inches apart, and zoysia sprigs are planted 6 inches apart. Sprigs can also be planted end to end in rows, rather than at spaced intervals.

The most difficult task when sprigging or spot or strip sodding is keeping the bare areas free of weeds until the grass fills in. This may take from only a few weeks for bermudagrass to two years for zoysia. The best tool for keeping weeds out in the interim is the time-honored hoe.

SPOT SEEDING

Chances are your lawn doesn't need a complete overhaul, but can get by with spot seeding. Maybe there are patches of different-textured grass throughout the lawn. Or you may find patches of weeds or bare soil. Before you sprinkle a box of grass seed over the problem area, you have to decide why the problem occurred. Otherwise, that patch will probably return, no matter how often you sow.

Monitor your lawn for a few weeks, and you should have some idea what's wrong. If you're lucky, it's a simple problem. Perhaps a hose leak causes water to puddle, encouraging weeds and diseases. Maybe it's a corner that is continually skipped when you fertilize. Or the trouble patch could be right where you pour fertilizer into the spreader, giving the soil an overdose. Was gasoline spilled there, or herbicide?

The grass could be worn by heavy traffic from your family, neighbors, or dogs. You have a few options in this case. Use a fence to divert traffic to a walkway. Put in a walk with stones, gravel, or concrete. Or try a tougher grass, one that's more tolerant of traffic.

Bare patches may also be caused by poor drainage or soil problems. The ground may be compacted, or just worn out. Try digging into it with a screwdriver. You should be able to plunge it all the way to the handle without resorting to a sledgehammer. If you can't, the soil is too compacted. For a fairly simple cure, work plenty of organic matter (compost, peat moss, or dried manure) into the area. Then stay off it. If this doesn't work, you may have to break through the subsoil and install a dry well. Use a spade or pickax if you run into rock-solid hardpan. The well should be at least

1 foot in diameter and 1 foot deep. Fill it with gravel to allow the water to drain out, cover with soil, and reseed.

Patches of extremely sandy or clayey soil may also show thin grass. The program is the same for both. Dig up the patch and add a 6-inch layer of organic matter.

If there are only a few troublesome patches, the problem is probably not fertility. However, a tree may drain fertility from the soil and cause a lackluster patch of lawn. Add a 2-inch layer of compost, or a thin layer of a high-nitrogen fertilizer such as bloodmeal. If shade is the culprit, either trim nearby trees and shrubs to allow more light through, or choose a shade-tolerant grass or groundcover for the spot.

Once you've diagnosed and corrected the problem, it's time to choose the seed for the doctored patches. It's helpful to know what the lawn is planted in because you want the new patch to blend in. The most important feature to match is texture. Coarse-textured grass in the middle of a fine-textured lawn will stick out like a sore thumb. You'd do as well to let weeds grow there instead.

If the patch is growing under different circumstances, such as shade or heavy traffic, you may have to plant a different grass. Otherwise, you want to match cul-tural requirements of the existing lawn—drought tolerance, fertilizer requirements, and so on. You don't want to add a hungry grass to a lawn that you intend to feed minimally. Nor do you want to add a grass that will turn brown with the first frost to a lawn that will stay green until the snow falls. Consult Chapter 2 to match a new grass with the old.

You've corrected the problem, you've bought the grass. Now it's time to plant. If there are any scattered grass plants or weeds growing in the patch, dig them out. Unless the soil is compacted, there's no need to dig up the entire patch. Just rough up the soil well with a rake, and wet it down with at least an inch of water. Give the water time to penetrate the soil. Scatter the seed at the rate recommended on the package, or refer to the table, How Much Seed Do You Need? on page 60. Then cover with a thin layer of topsoil, sand, or screened compost. Set up a sprinkler or soaker hose so you can keep the top of the soil evenly moist—but not drenched—until the grass germinates. Germination will be improved if you cover the area with a thin layer of straw mulch, burlap, or a spun-bonded row cover.

Just as with renovating and sodding, spot seeding should be done only at the right time for your area.

4

FEEDING THE LAWN

At the end of a long winter, most of us are feeling green-deprived. Forget the robins — the first true sign of spring is the greening of the lawn. The faster the greening, and the deeper the green, the better we feel. It satisfies our senses to be able to gaze at a long, green expanse of grass that's all our own. That explains the human phenomenon known as the spring suburban fertilizing frenzy.

You can witness it each spring as soon as the snow clears: Station wagons line up at the garden center, as customers haul out bag after bag of lawn fertilizer bearing names like Turf Blaster and Ultra-Green. Back home, they dump, spread, and scatter the stuff on their lawns, then stand back and watch the grass pop.

It works. Sure enough, the grass shoots up and turns so green it's almost blue. But weeds thrive along with the grass. Disease strikes. And the lawnmower barely has time to cool off before the grass needs cutting again. Even so, as soon as the grass begins to look the least bit pale, it's back to the garden center to load up again on fertilizer — spring, summer, and fall.

For years, turf experts encouraged that kind of behavior, but they've changed their tune. Finally, the official word is, "Enough is enough!"

OVERDOSED ON NITROGEN

Researchers have begun to realize that all the fertilizer is doing more harm than good. Massive doses are a waste of time and money. Studies at the department of agronomy at Alabama Polytechnic University showed that fully one half of all soluble nitrogen applied to the soil will be leached out and won't reach the plants. And even the half that *does* reach the grass plants may be hurting them.

"New research has led us to change the way we think about fertilizing lawns," says Eliot Roberts, director of the Lawn Institute, a seedmen's association. Multiple feedings of high-nitrogen fertilizer are out of style. "We've found that the grass plant is a very efficient user of nitrogen," he says. It works harder than was once thought, converting nitrogen into vigorous growth. It is, in short, fuel-efficient.

Babying the grass by pouring on fertilizer reduces that natural efficiency. "The more chemicals you use, the more you disturb the natural biological processes that convert organic matter into nutrients to keep the lawn going," Roberts says. It has been proven that excess fertilizer slows the action of microflora and microfauna. When they're not working up to speed, conversion of clippings slows to a halt. "Some of the best lawns I've seen are never fertilized, but they have an easy time converting clippings to nutrients," he says. "But once you get heavily involved with chemical fertilizers, you're increasing the growth rate of the plant and growing it to death."

LAZY GRASS

Apply too much fertilizer and you can be inviting insect and disease problems, says Judd Ringer of Ringer Research, which sells natural lawn and garden fertilizer by mail order from Eden Prairie, Minnesota. "Basically, people are overfertilizing their lawns. The nitrogen is available immediately to the roots, so the roots don't have to work to seek out nourishment. They grow on top and don't loosen the soil. Dinner is served at the top of the soil." A result is soil compaction, which leads to trouble with insects and diseases.

Ringer says the heavy use of nitrogen fertilizer can discourage beneficial aerobic organisms. That allows harmful microorganisms, many of which are anaerobic, to flourish. With fewer microorganisms to decompose roots, shoots, and clippings, thatch may build up.

Most synthetic fertilizers acidify the soil and slow down or kill off biological processes. A seven-year study at the Uni-

NO PENALTY FOR CLIPPINGS

Grass clippings are a good source of free fertilizer and an important part of a low-maintenance fertilizer schedule. They can provide up to one-half of the nitrogen needed by a lawn. Rake them up and you're robbing your turf of food, which you will have to replace.

Studies at the University of Connecticut Agricultural Experiment Station demonstrated the value of grass clippings. Researchers fertilized turf plots with 4 pounds of nitrogen per 1,000 square feet. The grass was mowed regularly (once a week in spring and fall, once every other week in summer) and clippings were collected, then weighed and analyzed for nitrogen content. A season's worth of clippings from a 1,000-square-foot plot contained 1.8 pounds of nitrogen, nearly one-half of the total applied as fertilizer.

In plots where the clippings were not raked up, the grass grew faster, making more clippings that contained more nitrogen, so that by the third year nearly 80 percent of the applied nitrogen had been returned to the plot via the clippings.

The study also dispelled the fear that leaving the clippings would lead to thatch buildup. By tracing the nitrogen with isotopes, researchers found that clippings begin to decompose almost immediately. Within a week after cutting, the nitrogen from the clippings began to show up in new growth of grass.

However, that rapid breakdown is dependent on a live and active soil system. Chemical fertilizers slow the activity of decomposers — earthworms, bacteria, fungi, and other microorganisms — and can stall the breakdown of clippings, causing thatch.

The only time you should routinely remove clippings is when converting from a chemical system, especially if you already have a thatch problem. You can also rake up clippings after the first mowing in the spring to help the grass green up and after the last fall mowing to reduce the chance of disease. Finally, remove clippings whenever you cut off more than one-half of the topgrowth.

versity of Kentucky showed that increasing annual nitrogen fertilization resulted in a significant decrease of pH. Five plots of Kentucky bluegrass were fertilized annually at rates equivalent to 1, 2, 3, 4, and 5 pounds of nitrogen per 1,000 square feet.

Thatch did not accumulate at the lowest fertilizer levels, but became a problem in the two most heavily fertilized plots. The thatch increased as the earthworm population decreased. At the highest fertilizer rates, there were 66 percent fewer earthworms than in unfertilized plots. The researchers suggest that the decrease was due to soil acidification and the reduction of calcium, which is important to earthworm metabolism.

"I maintain that a lot of insect and disease problems are caused by an imbalance of microbial activity," Ringer says. And tests at Michigan State University bear him out. "The dead roots are not breaking down," Ringer explains. "The lawn gets soft. You sink into it up to your ankles. There's excessive runoff. You have to water and fertilize more frequently. The lawn may look good for a year or two, but it's an artificial system, propped up by fertilizer and pesticides. It becomes a vicious cycle."

How do you break that cycle? Feed the soil, not the plant.

"A common approach for commercial companies is to focus on the plant, and get it green with intense fertilization," says Richard Hawk, of Green Pro Services. Green Pro is a New York-based natural lawn service company that also trains and supplies other applicators across the country. "The chemical lawn process only addresses the topgrowth," he says. "But the more intensive the culture, the more open it is to disease. No matter what they dump on, the grass will thrive for a while. But eventually the soil says no. In about three years the lawn peters out. Eventually, it will catch up with you. The soil will tattle on you sooner or later.

"Soil is money in the bank, and grass is the interest," Hawk says. "A lawn can only be as good as the soil."

CALL IN THE RESERVES

Slowly soluble, low-analysis natural fertilizers, like bloodmeal or organic mixes, feed the roots and allow the plants to make a good supply of carbohydrates. Carbohydrates are the energy source, the gas in the tank. They're the usable form of food created through fertilization and photosynthesis. Carbohydrates are especially important during times of stress, and the goal of fertilization is to build up carbohydrate reserves so the plant can keep growing steadily and vigorously. The rate at which carbohydrates are made depends in part on climate and mowing practices, but perhaps the most controllable factor is fertilization.

In the spring, heavy applications of nitrogen cause the grass to spurt. In its rapid growth, it draws on its carbohydrate reserves. Apply too much fertilizer and the grass may exhaust this supply. The grass gets hooked—dependent on more fertilization for growth. High-nitrogen fertilizers push the foliage into excessive growth, and repeated mowings cause carbohydrate reserves to be devoted to further growth and healing wounds. The trouble here is that carbohydrates that go to the blades can't go to the roots. The roots don't develop as they should, so when the hot, dry weather of summer arrives they're unable to dig deep for moisture.

In the summer, heavy fertilizer applications also increase respiration of the grass. That's not good for cool-season grasses, because they consume carbohydrates faster than photosynthesis can provide them. The grass weakens. But warm-season grasses

FERTILIZER SCHEDULE

Your fertilizer schedule will depend on where you live, the kind of grass you're growing, and what you want for your lawn. The following is a general calendar, offering low- and medium-maintenance schedules for the five grass zones. The actual doses will vary for each species. To find out the high and low doses for the species that grow in your lawn, see "Grasses' Nitrogen Needs" on page 73.

Zone 1: The Humid Northeast

Low-maintenance: Full low dose in September, October, or after grass stops growing actively

Medium-maintenance: ½ high dose in September or October; ½ in May or June after first rampant growth slows

Zone 2: The Humid South

For Summer Grasses

Low-maintenance: ½ low dose in June, ½ in August

Medium-maintenance: ¼ high dose every month, May to August

For Winter Grasses

Full low dose in September or October

Zone 3: The Great Plains

Low-maintenance: Full low dose in September

Medium-maintenance: ½ high dose in September, ½ in November; or ½ high dose in September, ¼ in November, ¼ in May

Zone 4: The Dry Southwest

For Summer Grasses, Cool-Season Species, Irrigated

½ high dose in October or November, ½ in May or June

For Summer Grasses, Warm-Season Species, Irrigated

¼ high dose every month, May to August

For Summer Grasses, Warm-Season Species, Non-Irrigated

½ low dose in April or May, ½ in August

For Winter Grasses, Cool-Season Species

Full low dose in October or November

Zone 5: The Humid Northwest

Low-maintenance: Full low dose in October, November, or after grass stops growing actively

Medium-maintenance: ½ high dose in October or November, ½ in May or June after first rampant growth slows

are more active photosynthesizers in hot weather, so they can continue to grow. Thus, summer fertilization encourages warm-season grasses over cool-season ones. That's fine for southern lawns, but in the North, warm-season grasses are undesirable. Some, like crabgrass, are weeds. High nitrogen levels in the summer give them an advantage in the northern lawn.

Southern lawns need summer fertilization, but for northern lawns, the best time to fertilize is fall. At that time of year, photosynthetic activity remains high, but cool temperatures slow topgrowth. The plants make more food than they can use. The carbohydrate level in plant tissue, shoots, and roots builds up and carries over into the spring, when it can be used to help the grass get off to a good start.

Warm-season grasses need fertilization during their peak growth period, starting in spring and continuing through summer. But don't fertilize too late into the growing season; fall fertilization encourages cool-season weeds in winter, and it can cause winter injury to cold-sensitive warm-season grasses.

Instant green and lush growth should not be the goal of a fertilizing program. The goal should be steady and vigorous growth, through building up carbohydrate reserves for times of stress.

GRASS NEEDS MORE THAN N

Though grass needs less packaged fertilizer than you might think, it still needs food, and a complete spectrum of it.

Nitrogen (N) gets all of the attention. For years, the alphabet of lawn fertilization began and ended with N. Look at a bag of lawn fertilizer in the store and you get the impression the other elements — phosphorus and potassium — are there just as fillers: You'll find 20-4-8, 27-3-9, 34-3-7, even 45-0-0. Any book on lawn care will give fertilizer recommendations in terms of so many pounds of nitrogen per 1,000 square feet, with no mention of the other macroelements (to say nothing of the micros).

Until about a decade ago, even turf experts were befuddled by the feeding habits of grass. They just didn't know what role phosphorus, potassium, and many of the other elements played in the growth of the grass plant.

NITROGEN

Now, a lot more is known about grass nutrition, and fertilizer recommendations are more sophisticated. Of course, nitrogen is still important. It's what gives you the most visible results. Nitrogen is fuel for the blades. It makes them grow and greens them up.

On the plus side, nitrogen makes sturdy, rapidly maturing, quick-spreading grass which fights weeds. Grass needs nitrogen most when the roots are growing more actively than the shoots. That's in spring and fall for cool-season grasses, and in spring and summer for warm-season grasses.

On the negative side, excessive nitrogen can cause shoots to grow too fast, making them succulent and tender, and outstripping the ability of their roots to

GRASSES' NITROGEN NEEDS

Pounds of actual nitrogen per 1,000 square feet per year, both low- and high-maintenance doses.

Species	Low	High
Bahiagrass	2	4
Bentgrass	2	4
Bermudagrass	1	4
Kentucky bluegrass	2	3
Buffalograss	1	2
Carpetgrass	2	3
Centipedegrass	2	4
Fine fescue	1	2
Tall fescue	1	2
Perennial ryegrass	2	3
St. Augustinegrass	2	4
Zoysiagrass	2	3

support them. Overextended grass is easy prey for diseases, especially brown patch, fusarium patch and fusarium blight, pythium, and powdery mildew.

Today, experts recommend a "moderate" amount of nitrogen, applied only once or twice a year for cool-season grasses, and three or four times a year for warm-season grasses. What does moderate mean? That depends on the grass species. For recommendations, see the table above. As a general guideline (or if you don't know what kind of grass you have), start with 2 pounds of nitrogen per 1,000 square feet per year,

applied in the fall in the North, and in the spring and fall in the South.

HERE TODAY, GONE TOMORROW

Synthetic lawn fertilizers are tempting. They're easy to buy and easy to use. They come premixed and bagged, and are available at every hardware store and garden center. But your lawn pays for that ease. Most of them contain the wrong kind of nitrogen.

There are two forms of nitrogen: water-soluble and water-insoluble. The solubility determines how fast the nitrogen becomes available in the soil. Water-soluble forms of nitrogen begin breaking down as soon as they hit the dirt. Water-insoluble fertilizers are released slowly through the chemical action of soil microorganisms.

Water-soluble fertilizers can give the grass a quick boost. But water carries them away, and they soon can be leached out of root range. The grass plants will pig out and put on a spurt of growth, but in a month they'll be hungry again and the nitrogen will be long gone. A single annual feeding of soluble nitrogen can't possibly satisfy a lawn.

Unfortunately, synthetic chemical lawn fertilizers are composed mostly of cheaper, soluble nitrogen. Next time you're in a hardware store, take a look at a bag of lawn food. The nitrogen will be listed as either soluble or insoluble. Chances are there will be far more of the first.

There are several types of synthetic chemical fertilizers available for turf. Most of them contain urea, with an analysis of 45 percent nitrogen. This is not a form of natural animal urine, but a synthetic substance, manufactured from air and natural gas or coal. Like natural urea, it can burn plants. Ureaform combines urea with formaldehyde, a suspected carcinogen that is also dangerous to bacterial life in the soil. Ammonium nitrate is another very strong, very soluble fertilizer that quickly leaches out of the soil.

STAYING POWER: THE ORGANIC ALTERNATIVE

"Natural, organic-type fertilizers are the best type to use because they are slow-acting," says Eliot Roberts of the Lawn Institute. "They include slow-release nitrogen, phosphorus, and potassium. This is how you get a lawn to grow slow enough so you don't kill yourself mowing it. People have to mow them so much because they use extra water and extra fertilizer, which keeps them growing fast all summer. You get a slow rate of growth by using natural, organic fertilizers."

Organic fertilizers are, for the most part, moderate in nitrogen content, neutral in pH, and water-insoluble—just what the lawn ordered. They are usually lower

NATURAL NITROGEN NUMBERS

Pounds of organic fertilizer needed to provide 1 pound of nitrogen per 1,000 square feet of lawn.

Fertilizer	Pounds
Alfalfa meal	10
Bloodmeal (10-0-0)	10
Castor pomace (5-1-1)	20
Cottonseed meal (7-2-1)	15
Erth-Rite (3-2-2)	34
Milorganite (6-2-0)	17
Mix 1 (4-5-4)	25
2 parts dried blood	
1 part rock phosphate	
4 parts wood ashes	
Mix 2 (2-4-2)	50
4 parts coffee grounds	
1 part bonemeal	
1 part wood ashes	
Nitro-10 (10-0-0)	10
Poultry manure (4-4-2)	25

in nitrogen than synthetic fertilizers and may be more expensive, pound for pound, in the short run. But as much as half of soluble fertilizer is washed away and wasted. And since natural fertilizers are kind to the lawn, you save the time and money that you would otherwise have to spend fighting insects, disease, and weeds.

To most of us, "organic fertilizers" means barnyards and manure. Animal manure is certainly the most available and the cheapest form of natural nitrogen. But not many of us are ready to spread fresh manure over our lawns. Besides putting us out of favor with our neighbors, fresh manure is just too bulky for turf applications.

Fortunately, there are plenty of other natural sources of nitrogen. You can find bags of dried cow manure at just about any garden center. Most brands are deodorized and easy to handle, but at only a 1 or 2 percent nitrogen content, this alternative is fairly expensive. Dried poultry manure is a better value, packing up to 5 percent nitrogen. One 40- or 50-pound bag of dried poultry manure will feed 1,000 square feet of lawn per year. Poultry manure is not odorless, but the smell dissipates rapidly once it has been spread.

Other options include bloodmeal, cottonseed meal, fish emulsion, leather tankage, and mixed organic fertilizers. See the table on page 74 for a list of organic fertilizers and application rates.

THE FORGOTTEN FIVE

The other five macronutrients — phosphorus, potassium, calcium, magnesium, and sulfur — don't get as much attention as nitrogen, but they are just as important. Turfgrass needs just a little of them, but it needs that little nonetheless. A balanced natural fertilizer will provide them in adequate amounts. But if you have been using high-nitrogen fertilizers or none at all, there may be an imbalance in your soil. A soil test will tell you if you're low and how much of these macronutrients to add.

PHOSPHORUS

Phosphorus (P) works behind the scenes and under the ground. Young turf needs a good supply of it. In a fertilizer, it helps seeds to germinate and turf to estab-

HOW MUCH DO YOU NEED?

It's easy to figure the application rates for organic lawn fertilizers. All you need to know is the analysis of the fertilizer and the grass's requirements in pounds of nitrogen per 1,000 square feet. The three numbers in the analysis of a fertilizer are the percentages of nitrogen, phosphorus, and potassium in the substance. So a 50-pound bag of 4-2-1 fertilizer contains 4 percent nitrogen, 2 percent phosphorus, and 1 percent potassium. To figure the actual content, convert the analysis number to decimals, in this case 0.04, 0.02, and 0.01. Then multiply the decimals by the weight of the bag to get the actual weight of nutrients. In this example, when you multiply each of these decimal figures times 50 you get 2 pounds of nitrogen, 1 pound of phosphorus, and ½ pound of potassium. You'll need a half bag, or 25 pounds, of fertilizer to put down 1 pound of nitrogen.

MILORGANITE

Milorganite may be everything you need in a lawn fertilizer. For over 60 years, it has been used on hundreds of golf courses across the country, even where "organic" is an unknown word. Milorganite is a dried sewage sludge product from the Milwaukee Metropolitan Sewage District. It is purified by heat and microorganisms to reduce heavy metal content.

Early in 1987, there was concern that heavy metals (primarily cadmium) in Milorganite were connected to Lou Gehrig's disease (amyotrophic lateral sclerosis), but subsequent studies show that this is not true. Milorganite contains 2.1 parts per million of cadmium. That means a 40-pound bag contains only $\frac{1}{1000}$ of an ounce of the heavy metal. To exceed the acceptable cadmium intake limit, a person would have to inhale or ingest between 1½ and 6 pounds of Milorganite per year.

Along with a 6-2-0 analysis, Milorganite contains sulfur, calcium, magnesium, iron, zinc, boron, copper, manganese, and molybdenum. "In my book, I have not found anything better for lawn care than Milorganite," says Eliot Roberts, director of the Lawn Institute. "Talk with golf superintendents around the country and I bet you'll find a high percentage of them use Milorganite as a prime fertilizer for their golf greens."

lish quickly and strongly. For established grass, phosphorus aids in root growth.

Phosphorus is taken in by ion exchange at the root surface. It is present in every plant cell, where it is used for transforming other elements into energy.

To maintain an adequate level of soil phosphorus, you need to add only ½ pound per 1,000 square feet per year. You can provide that with just 5 pounds of bonemeal or 2 to 3 pounds of soft rock phosphate per 1,000 square feet. If your initial soil test reads low to very low, double or quadruple the amount the first year. Other organic sources of phosphorus are fish emulsion, sludge, bloodmeal, and cottonseed meal.

POTASSIUM

Potassium (K) is suddenly being called the miracle element. Only lately have agronomists begun to get a clear idea of how much it does for the grass plant. Potassium's work doesn't show up dramatically in color, growth, or density, but it has been proven to toughen the turf. It makes grass more resistant to heat, cold, drought, disease, and traffic. Only a little potassium is needed to work these miracles — about one-half to two-thirds the normal nitrogen rate, or 1 to 2 pounds of potassium per 1,000 square feet per year. That's about 15 to 25 pounds of greensand or granite dust, or 10 to 20 pounds of wood ashes.

If you've left out the potassium in previous years while using high-nitrogen fertilizers, you may have to add more to start. Should your soil test read *very* low in potassium, add 3½ pounds (about 50 pounds of greensand or granite dust) per 1,000 square feet. Add 2 to 2¼ if the reading is not quite so low. Other good natural sources of potassium are, in order from high to low by percentage, tobacco waste, dried sheep manure, millet, and buckwheat straw.

CALCIUM, MAGNESIUM, AND SULFUR

Calcium (Ca) is another nutrient that is beginning to get some attention. Recent studies have shown that it helps by improving the uptake of nitrogen and increasing the growth of root hairs. The result is better overall quality, including color. This nutrient is also necessary for cell division.

You can provide calcium with dolomitic limestone. That will also supply magnesium (Mg), a constituent of chlorophyll that plays an important role in photosynthesis and helps the plant absorb phosphorus.

Sulfur (S) is a nutrient you shouldn't have to worry about unless you've been using high-nitrogen fertilizers. It improves grass color, increases carbohydrate reserves, and contributes to cold tolerance, protein synthesis, and new growth. Powdery mildew is more prevalent when sulfur is low. To correct deficient soils, apply elemental sulfur at a rate of ½ pound per 1,000 square feet.

MICRONUTRIENTS

Grass needs a good supply of micronutrients to grow vigorously. A balanced natural fertilizer program will supply them all. But a lawn that has been overfed with chemical fertilizers may show imbalances.

Iron (Fe) is essential for the formation of chlorophyll. It improves fall and winter color, enhances root development, and reduces the effects of stress. Excess phosphorus creates an iron deficiency, and wet or cold soils contribute to the problem. Greensand and Milorganite (processed sludge) are good sources of iron.

Manganese (Mn) activates photosynthesis. Deficiencies are most often found in alkaline soils. A light mulch of shredded alfalfa hay will contribute manganese.

Grass requires only minute amounts of zinc (Zn), but compaction, irrigation, and alkalinity reduce zinc availability. Dried manure is a good source.

Copper (Cu) is also needed in only small amounts. It can be provided with sawdust.

Boron (Bo) is used in protein synthesis and helps to maintain water balance in the plants. It's most plentiful in the tips of grass. Granite dust is a good source.

Molybdenum (Mb) is essential in nitrogen utilization. It can be supplied by phosphate rock.

THE WONDERS OF SEAWEED

Micronutrients should not be added unless a soil test indicates deficiencies. The great thing about an organic lawn care system is that you never have to worry

DEFICIENCY CHECKLIST

What at first may appear to be a disease can be caused by deficiencies of nutrients. Here are symptoms to look for. Unlike diseases, the symptoms will not appear in patches or spots, but over all or most of the lawn.

Nutrient	Deficiency Symptoms	Cure
Nitrogen	Light green or yellow-green leaves; may start dying at the tips	Add organic matter; bloodmeal; poultry manure
Phosphorus	Thin sod; thin, curled leaves; dusky blue-green with purple tint in cool weather	Adjust pH; add rock phosphate or bonemeal
Potassium	Yellow tips on leaves; may turn brown and die at the tips	Add wood ashes; greensand
Calcium	Reddish-brown leaves; may curl and die	Add lime for acid soils; add gypsum for alkaline soils
Magnesium	Yellow stripes on leaves, turning red	Add dolomitic limestone for acid soils; add Epsom salts (magnesium fate) for alkaline soils
Sulfur	Yellow leaves	Add rock phosphate; gypsum; elemental sulfur
Copper	Yellow and stunted leaves; tips die	Add copper sulfate; reduce nitrogen fertilization
Iron	Pale leaves, turning yellow	Add iron sulfate or chelated iron; reduce phosphorus fertilization
Zinc	Small and yellow leaves	Add zinc sulfate or zinc chelates
Molybdenum	Yellow and withered leaves	Add lime for acid soils
Manganese	Yellow spots on leaves; withered at tips	Add manganese sulfate
Boron	Slow growth; pale green tips; bronze tint	Add borax

about micronutrients. Most organic fertilizers are full of them. But if you want to be sure to get the most from your lawn, you can use seaweed, either liquid or granular. Seaweed contains as many as 50 important elements, including such micronutrients as boron, chlorine, copper, iron, manganese, molybdenum, and zinc. It also contains carbohydrates and protein. And in seaweed, the whole is even greater than the sum of its parts. That's because it is a catalyst that helps plants take up nutrients from other sources. It enhances the formation of plant hormones that are vital to growth, particularly of roots. And the trace elements and hormones in seaweed make grass green up fast.

Studies at Clemson University in South Carolina have shown that auxins produced by seaweed give plants increased resistance to some fungal diseases, including fusarium. Clemson's H. L. Senn conducted experiments with seaweed as a lawn fertilizer, and that's what he continues to use on his home lawn.

"I am very impressed with seaweed," Dr. Senn says. "In the trials, there was a reduction in the nematode populations. There was less fusarium and other wilts in the grass." And that's not all. "The grass was greener, more luxurious, and had a healthier appearance to it," Senn adds. "And it was able to survive stress better, withstanding extremely dry conditions and cold weather."

Senn found that 5 gallons per acre per season was a good rate for Maxicrop, a brand of seaweed. For smaller areas, that works out to just under a pint, about 15 ounces, per 1,000 square feet. At home, Senn makes a minimum of three applications per season. "I like to get it on early in the spring," he says, "in March before the grass greens up." He applies more in July when the weather warms and the lawn begins to brown. "And then again on the first of August to help it get ready for fall."

Dr. Senn dilutes Maxicrop at the standard rate of 7½ ounces to 100 gallons of water and applies it with either a backpack sprayer or siphon proportioner (described on page 82). He likes to supplement the seaweed with one or two applications of Nitro-10, at the standard rate. Senn says that the seaweed makes other fertilizers more effective, acting as a chelating agent so that nutrients are more available to the plants.

AN ORGANIC SUCCESS STORY

At Davidson College in North Carolina, groundskeeper Irvin Brawley has proven that an organic system can work in a big way. He manages about 100 acres of lawn and athletic fields, and he does it all organically. Liquid seaweed is a part of his program.

Brawley says his success starts with organic fertilizers. Because the college is in the transition zone, Brawley maintains both warm-season and cool-season grasses, and has developed natural fertilizer programs for both. He began gardening organically at home 12 years ago. Organic techniques worked so well there that he began to wonder if they would work on the college grounds. "So I took the money I normally spent on chemical fertilizer and bought organic fertilizer," he says.

First, Brawley made sure that the soil was the proper pH: "The main thing is to get your pH right for the type of grass you want to grow." Fescues and bentgrasses grow best in a range of 6.5 to 7, while bluegrass, ryegrass, and bermudagrass pre-

SWEET OR SOUR SOIL?

The acidity of the soil is critical. Unless it is correct, fertilizers will have relatively little effect. When the soil is too alkaline (pH above 8.5) or too acid (pH below 5.5), many of the nutrients are locked up and unavailable.

When the pH gets much higher than 7, iron, zinc, manganese, and copper become unavailable. Toward the other end of the scale, when the pH dips below 6, phosphorus availability is reduced, and calcium and magnesium are depleted. For nutrient availability, the best range is slightly acid to neutral, 6 to 7. At higher or lower rates, microorganism activity slows or even stops, reducing the breakdown of organic matter and the consequent release of nitrogen, sulfur, and other nutrients. You can pour on all the fertilizer you want, but it will never get to the plants.

A soil test will indicate the pH of your soil, with recommendations to correct the level.

To Raise pH				To Lower pH		
(Pounds of limestone needed per 1,000 square feet to raise pH to 6.5 in three soil types)				(Pounds of sulfur needed per 1,000 square feet to lower pH to 6.5 in two soil types)		
Soil pH	Sand	Loam	Clay	Soil pH	Sand	Clay
4.5	50	135	195	8.5	45	70
5.0	40	105	155	8.0	30	45
5.5	30	80	110	7.5	10	20
6.0	15	40	55			

fer a slightly higher pH. "That lime is probably going to be the most beneficial additive you ever put on," he says.

Next, he mixed up his own batch of organic fertilizer. For nitrogen, Brawley uses Fertrell's Nitro-10, a leather-making byproduct. He says other good nitrogen sources are cottonseed meal, bloodmeal, and composted manure. He uses rock phosphate to provide phosphorus and greensand for potassium. He mixes them to make a 10-10-10 fertilizer, with 7½ pounds of Nitro-10, 2½ pounds of rock phosphate, and 10¾ pounds of greensand. That's enough to cover 1,000 square feet of lawn.

For his cool-season grasses, Brawley makes two applications per year. "The best time to apply fertilizer, without a doubt, is in the fall," he says. Next best is the spring, so he makes two applications per year.

His fertilizer schedule for warm-season grasses is a little more involved. He makes two applications of the homemade 10-10-10 at the same rate as the cool-season mix— one in early May, the other late in September. He supplements this with a topdressing of nitrogen—½ pound actual nitrogen, or 5 pounds of Nitro-10 per 1,000 square feet.

Brawley suggests that homeowners can save themselves a lot of mixing and figuring by buying blended organic fertilizer such as Erth-Rite or Fertrell, and applying it according to the recommended rate. But the best lawn aid of them all, he says, might be homemade compost. And yet of the tons he makes each year, all go on the flower beds—he hasn't yet figured out a way to grind it fine enough to top-dress the lawns. "If you could compost enough, grind and top-dress with it, that compost could serve as your fertilizer, almost completely," he says.

USING A SPREADER

Although you can broadcast fertilizer by the handful, or shoot it out with a rotary spreader, drop spreaders (also called band spreaders) are the most accurate way to apply lawn fertilizer. That's especially true with organic fertilizers, because their particles are usually not as uniform in size or shape as those in chemical fertilizer.

Drop spreaders are bins on wheels. They have an adjustable opening at the bottom that sifts fertilizer to the ground as you push them along. A control, either on the bin or the handle, allows you to vary the rate of application. The control is usually marked with standard numbers. Most chemical fertilizers have spreader setting recommendations on the bag. Some organic fertilizers do too. For Milorganite, for example, you're instructed to set the spreader setting at number 10. But for most natural fertilizers, like bloodmeal and cottonseed meal, you're on your own. You'll have to do some experimenting to get the right application rate.

For starters, mark off a 1,000-square-foot area on your lawn. Then figure out how many pounds of fertilizer you want to spread. If you intend to apply 1 pound of nitrogen per 1,000 square feet, and you're using composted chicken manure with an analysis of 4-4-2, you'll need 25 pounds.

Fill the spreader with more fertilizer than you need—double the amount, if the spreader will hold it. So with 50 pounds of chicken manure in the spreader, set the selector at the lowest setting, and push the

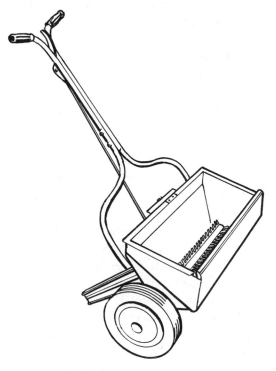

Drop spreaders have an adjustable gate that allows you to set the correct fertilizer application rate.

spreader over the marked-off area, walking at a normal pace.

When you've finished, empty the remaining fertilizer into a bag and weigh it. Subtract that figure from the number of pounds you started with to figure out how much you've applied. If you have 25 pounds left, in this case, you've applied exactly the right amount. If you've applied less than the desired amount, set the gate wider and try again on another spot. In the unlikely event that you've applied too much fertilizer at the lowest setting, your only option is to quicken your pace while pushing the spreader.

When using a drop spreader, make sure to overlap each pass slightly so you don't leave any unfertilized spots, and don't stop without closing the gate.

The easiest way to apply liquid fertilizer such as seaweed concentrate or fish emulsion is through a lawn sprinkler. You'll need a quality sprinkler with even coverage —preferably an adjustable oscillating sprinkler that covers up to 3,000 square feet—and a siphon proportioner (Hozon is a common brand). The inexpensive siphon screws on between the hose bib and the hose. A small hose goes from the siphon to a bucket. When you turn on the faucet, water flows through the siphon and sucks liquid up from the bucket. It mixes the contents of the bucket with the tap water at a proportion of about 1 to 15 or 1 to 20, depending on water pressure.

For normal lawn care, you should apply 1 cup of seaweed concentrate per 1,000 square feet twice a year. Mix the cup of seaweed with 1 gallon of water in a bucket (use 2 cups and 2 gallons of water to cover 2,000 square feet, 3 cups and 3 gallons for 3,000, and so on). Place the siphon hose in the bucket, and turn on the faucet. In about five minutes, the siphon will have drained the fertilizer mix. Run the sprinkler for another five minutes to thoroughly mois-ten the grass, and the job is done.

Fish emulsion contains more nitrogen than seaweed, so it should be applied in a weaker solution. Try 2 ounces per gallon of water per 1,000 square feet. If you see no reaction, double the amount for the next application.

5

THE ART OF MOWING

Mowing is the most important thing you will ever do to your lawn. It could be the most harmful or the most beneficial. Yet few of us understand how to do the job. Probably the extent of your lessons was the time your father showed you how to start the mower and pointed you in the direction of the front yard.

If you're an average American home-owner, you spend 40 hours a year behind a lawnmower. Chances are, your technique falls under one of a couple of mowing styles: You mow every week, at the same time and in the same way; or you wait until your backyard begins to look like a savannah, and mow only when you begin to lose things in it.

In fact, a rigid mowing schedule doesn't suit the grass. That may come as a surprise to you if your routine is to mow at the same time every week, in the same way and in the same direction. From spring until the snow flies, millions of Americans will be cranking up their lawnmowers like clockwork. They'll mow on schedule week in and week out, regardless of heat, drought, floods, or frost.

There's a lot more to mowing than that. Just because it's Saturday doesn't mean it's time to mow the lawn. Grass grows at different rates through the year. And it doesn't want to be mowed at the same height every time. Several factors should influence your mowing schedule: water, heat, fertilizer, disease, dormancy, and seasonality. The right way to mow your lawn in the spring may be precisely the wrong way to do it in the fall.

How and when you mow will have an impact on the health and appearance of your lawn—its vigor, disease resistance, weediness, and water and fertilizer requirements. Properly done, mowing can kill weeds, cure diseases, save water, and provide fertilizer. Spend a little time figuring out the best schedule for your mowing, and you will save yourself a lot of work later on in the season.

Even the experts are still learning about the effects of clipping on grass. The science of mowing is fairly young. Before 1830, the few existing lawns were kept trim either by scythe or sheep. In the Middle Ages, most lawns were "flowery medes," or patches of wildflower-sprinkled sod brought in from pasture. Low maintenance was the order of the day—the grass was mowed just twice a year—because a lawn took

days to mow by hand, not hours. The reel lawnmower came along in 1830, and by 1900 it had acquired a motor. Summer Saturday mornings haven't been the same since.

But advances in mowing technology haven't changed one fact—mowing is an unnatural thing to do. Your lawn does not want to be mowed. It would prefer to keep growing straight up, to mature and set seeds. In this regard, the wishes of the lawn and the lawn owner are at odds. We've come to think that a closely cropped lawn looks good. Even the smell of freshly mown grass suits us. There's something about a trimmed lawn that pleases the senses. The shorter it is, the better we feel. But that close cut

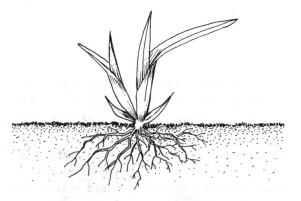

Grass can withstand mowing because the growing point is at the crown near the soil line, not at the tip of the blade.

doesn't do much for the lawn, and we, the lawn mowers, pay for it in the long run with more work, more sickly grass, and a balky, hard-to-manage lawn.

The art of mowing involves striking a delicate balance between an attractive lawn and a healthy lawn. This means investing more thought than simply dragging out the mower every Saturday from May to October. At times you may have to raise or lower the height of the mower deck. Sometimes you'll mow twice a week, while at other periods of the season you may have to get the mower out only twice a month.

To understand your lawn's changing needs, it helps to know how grass plants grow. Grasses are basal-growing crops. That's why you can cut off their tops without killing them. The growing point is not at the tip of each blade, but at the crown of the plant, near the soil line. The tips are not the youngest parts of the plant, but among the oldest. Cut them off and new growth pushes up from the crown—sometimes all too quickly to suit us.

THE GOOD AND BAD OF MOWING

When the mower prunes those grass tips, the plant undergoes a lot of changes, some of them good, but most of them not. Norman Hummel, assistant professor of turfgrass science at Cornell University in New York, puts it dramatically. "Mowing is a violent physical removal of living tissue,"

he says, "causing a severe shock to the grass plant." The shock results primarily from a sudden and severe reduction of the food available to the plant. Grass, like all green plants, lives mostly on food manufactured in its leaves rather than drawn up from the roots.

Through the process of photosynthesis, the blades use energy from sunlight to combine carbon, oxygen, and hydrogen into sugars, starches, and fibers. The sugars then combine with soil minerals to make proteins, plant oils, and fats. But these soil minerals make up only 5 percent of the solid material in the grass plant. The balance is the carbon, hydrogen, and oxygen which the blades take from the air. Cut those blades, and you reduce the ability of the plant to manufacture food.

The food manufactured by the leaves is used for both topgrowth and root growth. The longer the topgrowth, the deeper the roots; so, the shorter you cut your grass, the less the roots will grow. That can be very important to the health of your lawn, because a plant with deep roots will be better able to withstand drought and fight off diseases. Strong roots also serve to store food that has been manufactured in the leaves.

Every time the grass is cut, the root system is weakened to some degree. When the grass is cut severely—more than 40 percent—the roots stop growing. The closer you cut, the longer it will take the roots to resume growing. Cut too close, and the roots may never grow again.

Food production is not the only thing at stake. Every time you mow the grass, you

A dull mower blade will shred grass blades, opening ports of entry for disease.

tear the plant (especially if the mower blade is not sharp) and create ports of entry for disease. Finally, close cutting allows sunlight to both dry the soil and encourage weed seeds to germinate.

Mowing is not all bad news for grass. Properly done, it can make a lawn thicker and more weed-resistant. Here's why.

Like every other plant, grasses live to reproduce. Left to its own devices, a lawn grows until it sets seed. But mowing prevents sexual reproduction by seed formation, and many grasses respond by "tillering" — reproducing asexually, through the spread of stolons and rhizomes. The result is a thicker lawn.

Mowing encourages tillering because the blade tips contain chemicals that inhibit the growth of sideshoots. This works much like pruning a houseplant: Pinch off the terminal bud, and sideshoots grow. Mowing also allows more light to penetrate the lawn and give those young tillers a chance to develop.

Mowing height has been found to influence the spread of a new lawn. This was clearly demonstrated in trials at Purdue University in Indiana. Researchers there seeded three plots with Kentucky bluegrass and mowed them at different heights: ¾ inch, 1½ inches, and 3 inches. They measured the amount of ground covered by the bluegrass under the various treatments. After 22 weeks the ¾-inch lawn covered only 42 percent of the ground, while the 1½-inch lawn covered 64 percent of the ground, and the 3-inch lawn covered 80 percent.

Mower height is critical to mowing with the least harm. Perhaps you've heard the lawn mowing maxim, "Don't cut off any more than one-third of the height of the grass." In fact, tests have shown that four-tenths is the magic figure. Cut off more than that at any *one* time and the grass will be damaged.

TIME FOR A TRIM

The other mowing variable is frequency of cut. You have four choices: mowing close and often, close and infrequently, high and often, or high and infrequently.

The first option, mowing close and often, produces several negative effects. Plants are less able to synthesize and store

LAWN RESCUE

A single heavy mowing can literally shock a lawn to death. For example, suppose a lawn is left unattended over a month's vacation, so that it grows to 6 inches in height. When the family returns, the mower is cranked up and the lawn is cut back to just 1 inch. The grass tries to recover: It sends out a spurt of new growth, but this exhausts the food stores in the roots.

The grass literally may grow itself to death because there's too little surface area to manufacture enough new food to sustain it. The crowns, suddenly exposed to the sun after having been shaded by the tall growth, are sensitive to sunburn. What's more, the sudden removal of shade encourages the germination of crabgrass and other annual weed seeds on the surface of the soil. Finally, unless the plentiful clippings are raked up, they will form thatch and thereby encourage disease and prevent water from penetrating to the soil.

There are alternatives short of hiring someone to mow the lawn while you're gone. Mow gradually when you return. Cut no more than 1 inch off with the first mowing. Allow the grass to recover for a day or two, then cut off another inch. Continue cutting an inch at a time until you reach the desired height.

carbohydrates, they have decreased shoot density and leaf width (meaning a thinner lawn), and their root growth is slowed. You're better off mowing less often, with a higher setting of the lawnmower.

A test of clipping heights and frequencies of 'Merion' Kentucky bluegrass, conducted at the Michigan Agricultural Station, turned up some interesting suggestions for lawn management. Grass was grown with 14-hour daylengths, and day and night temperatures of 73° and 61°F. Plots were clipped at 1 and 2½ inches at three intervals: twice a week, once a week, and once every other week. The researchers then measured root weight, shoot regrowth, lateral stems, the root-to-shoot ratio, and photosynthesis.

They found that grass clipped at the higher height had greater root growth and shoot regrowth, and more lateral stems. Take these results out of the laboratory and it means this: Higher clipping makes healthier grass with deeper roots, more mass for photosynthesis (requiring less feeding by the lawn owner), and more tillers for a thicker sod (which means less weed invasion).

Every lawn owner would like to hear that the every-other-week clipping produced the best results. Unfortunately, that wasn't the case. The twice-weekly clipping produced more tillers and a greater root-to-shoot ratio. That's presumably because frequent mowing removes less tissue each time you mow. However, the height seemed to be more significant than the frequency. *Mowing high is the key,* no matter how often it is done.

So, how often and how high should you mow? The answers change with the time of the season, because grass grows at different rates throughout the spring, summer, and fall. Your mowing schedule should be set up with that in mind. The key is to mow less often when the roots are growing slowly. The roots of *cool-season grasses* grow fastest in late fall and early spring. They grow slowest in summer, and there may even be a natural root deterioration then. Fewer tillers will be produced as well. So this is when the greatest care must be taken in mowing. Cooler weather will bring renewed topgrowth, followed by increased root growth. Tillering increases, and rhizomes emerge from the soil. Root growth may continue after topgrowth stops, on into the winter. *Warm-season grasses* will show a similar pattern, though root growth occurs steadily through the summer.

Temperature plays an important role in how much you should mow. The warmer the weather, the less you should cut. Grasses that are already stressed by heat and drought can ill afford the stress of mowing.

Fortunately for northern lawn owners, their grasses need less mowing in the summer. Ideal mowing heights vary from species to species, and mowing heights for a single species can vary considerably according to climate. In the South, fine-leaved fescues and bluegrasses should be maintained at a 3-inch height. But in the North, especially at high altitudes where the nights are cool and the soil never heats up, they can be mowed regularly as low as ½ inch, though it's not clear why anyone would want to mow them that low.

As mentioned, species vary considerably in how they should be mowed. Some must be cut short: In fact, putting greens of bentgrass, fine-leaved fescues, and bermudagrass will tolerate ¼-inch mowing daily. If they're left to grow to 1 inch and mowed infrequently, hot weather can wipe them out. Tall-growing bermudagrass and buffalograss won't tolerate mowing below 1 inch. Tall fescues and ryegrasses take to mowing less kindly than other types. They should be mowed to 3 inches whenever they reach 4 inches.

A MOWING SCHEDULE

You may not want to hear this, but you can start mowing earlier than you thought in the spring, even before the grass turns green. By mowing off the brown tips of the grass, you allow more sunlight to reach the crowns and encourage strong early growth.

So, get the mower out as soon as the lawn dries. Adjust the mower deck so that you'll be cutting off about ½ inch of the grass. Rake up the clippings when you're done. Don't mow again until the grass turns green and begins growing actively. Check the table on page 91 to find the maximum mowing height for your grass. When your lawn reaches that height, set the mower ½ inch lower than your maximum mowing height and mow. For example, the maximum height for Kentucky bluegrass is 3 inches; set the mower at 2½ inches, and mow when the grass reaches 3 inches.

MOWING HEIGHTS

Here are the best mowing heights, in inches, by species. As indicated, the mower deck should be raised in hot weather or shade, and lowered for the last mow before winter.

Cool-Season Grasses	Cool Weather and/or Shade	Hot Weather	Last Mow
Creeping bentgrass	1⅓	⅔	⅓
Velvet bentgrass	¼	½	¼
Annual bluegrass	½	1	½
Canada bluegrass	3	4	3
Kentucky bluegrass	2½	3	2
Rough bluegrass	1	1½	½
Smooth bromegrass	3	4	3
Fine fescue	1½	2½	1
Tall fescue	2½	4	2
Annual ryegrass	2	2½	2
Perennial ryegrass	1½	2½	1
Warm-Season Grasses			
Bahiagrass	2	3	1½
Bermudagrass	½	1	½
Buffalograss	1½	2½	1
Carpetgrass	1	2	1
Centipedegrass	1	2	1
St. Augustinegrass	2	3	1½
Zoysiagrass	½	1	½

A QUICK MOWING GUIDE

You may need a ruler at first, but you'll soon be able to eyeball when the grass is high enough to be mowed. To get started, make a simple guide. Mark a wooden stake with these measurements: A line 2 inches from the bottom will be the soil line when the stake is sunk into the ground; then measure up to the normal mowing height (e.g., 3 inches for Kentucky bluegrass) and put another mark for that height plus one-third (in this case 4 inches). Stick one or two guide stakes in the lawn. When the grass reaches the top mark, it's time to mow. You can make other stakes for other times and places — hot weather, fall weather, shady spots, and so on.

Continue mowing at that spring height, just below maximum, until summer arrives. When temperatures reach the 80s consistently (in the North) or when more than two weeks pass without at least an inch of rain, it's time to raise the mower to the maximum height and reduce the frequency. You'll find that growth slows, unless it's artificially maintained by fertilizer and water, so you'll have to mow less frequently to keep that top third trimmed. Then, with the cooler temperatures and heavier rainfall of late summer, northern lawn grasses will begin another growth spurt. Reduce the mower height by ½ inch and mow more frequently. Finally, grass growth slows to a stop in fall: For your last mow of the season, reduce the height another ½ inch, and rake up the clippings.

For warm-season grasses, the principle is the same. Mow high in times of heat and drought to cause less stress and to encourage deep root growth. But warm-season grasses do not go dormant during the summer. They keep growing energetically, and require you to keep mowing high and frequently. Because they grow slowly during cool weather, you don't have to mow as often, but the mower should be set slightly higher in early spring and late fall to protect against freezing stress.

You should remove clippings after the first spring and last fall mowings to discourage diseases. But should you rake them up after every mowing? No. Clippings do not, as once believed, cause thatch, unless they are exceptionally long. That's because they start breaking down soon after they hit the ground.

In the process, they return a lot of nitrogen to the lawn, according to researchers at the University of Connecticut Agricultural Experiment Station. They found that grass clippings began to decompose in one week. "And within two weeks, nitrogen from the grass clippings could be found in new grass," reports Dr. Charles R. Frink, head of the experiment station's soil and water department. "By the end of the third year, we estimated that one-third of the nitrogen on the plots came from grass clippings," he notes. The researchers estimated that the grass clippings contributed about 1.8 pounds of nitrogen per 1,000 square feet.

The Connecticut researchers removed clippings from some plots and left them on others. Both plots had been fertilized with nitrogen in the spring and fall. "You didn't need any fancy instruments to see the difference," Dr. Frink says. "Where the clippings were left, the plots were much greener."

So raking and bagging clippings is a tremendous waste of resources. Clippings are free food. People who don't use them have to buy fertilizer to keep their lawns healthy.

Should you mow when the grass is wet? Preferably not. The lawnmower is one of the prime culprits in spreading disease spores, especially when the grass is wet. The mower also produces clumps of wet grass that decompose slowly and may smother the lawn below. Finally, a mower is likely to make ruts in a soggy lawn.

REEL OR ROTARY

Your mowing schedule also should be influenced by the type of mower you use. Forty or 50 years ago you had only one choice, the reel mower, either powered or push. And the push mower wasn't much different from the first lawnmowers of a century before. Since World War II, the rotary mower has roared onto the scene and driven the reel near extinction. The only reel mowers you'll see these days are huge ones on estates and golf courses, and small hand-powered ones on city lots.

And yet a reel mower cuts more kindly. Its blades sever the grass with a scissoring action, which creates a smaller cut area and slows evaporation in hot weather. A rotary, however, uses the speed of the whirring blade to chop the grass. If the blade is nicked or dull, the grass can be tattered and bruised. This opens ports of entry for

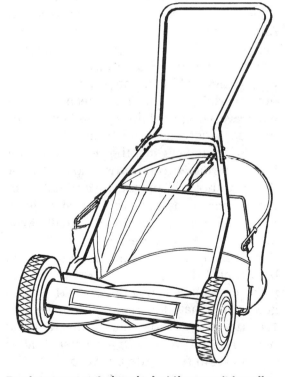

Reel mowers cut cleanly, but they can't handle tall grass or weeds.

disease, and in severe cases will give the entire lawn a grayish cast.

But reel mowers can be cranky machines, requiring repeated adjustment between blades and the cutting bed. And they are less versatile. They will cut low — and excel when clipping as close as ¼ inch — but they have trouble with anything over 2 inches. What's more, a reel mower will pass right over tough, stalky weeds without cutting them. Plantain stalks and seed heads, for example, will still be standing tall after a pass with a reel mower. These machines are useless in high grass or weeds. They can't be used to reclaim or tame a weedy area, as a rotary mower can. Another drawback is that they don't shred clippings as thoroughly as rotary mowers. Nor do they throw clippings to the side, where they can be further chopped on the next pass. When making a deep cut they will leave a carpet of thick grass behind the mower, which can contribute to thatch.

Reel mowers are the best choice for fine, well-manicured lawns, and should be the only choice if you're growing bentgrass, which has to be kept mowed at ¼ inch. Push reel mowers are fine for small lawns of less than 1,000 square feet.

Reel mowers vary in their number of blades and the number of cuts made per yard. Professional machines used on golf greens may have ten blades and make over 100 cuts per yard for a fine, clean cut. Most home reel mowers have five or six blades and make 40 to 70 cuts per yard.

Rotary mowers operate on a different principle than the reel machines. The rotary blade, spinning at up to 130 miles per hour, shatters as much as cuts the grass. It's a brutal process, and if the blade is the least bit dull it will damage the grass. How sharp is sharp enough? On golf courses where rotary mowers are in constant use, the blades are routinely sharpened every day. Once a month should be about right for the homeowner.

If they are kept sharp, rotary mowers are the best choice for the low-maintenance lawn. They can cut well at many heights, and can be used to clear weedy and overgrown areas.

What size mower do you need? Widely available cutting widths run from 18 to 24 inches. You'd be surprised by how much difference a couple of inches makes in the work you have to put into mowing. As an example, take a 1-acre lawn, mowed with a 4-inch overlap on each pass. If you mowed it with an 18-inch machine, you would make 171 swaths — a hike of 6.9 miles behind that mower. At an average speed of three miles per hour, that means you'd be investing two hours and 18 minutes to mow the lawn. But with a 21-inch mower, you'd cut 141 swaths, traveling 5.7 miles in one hour and 54 minutes. Move up to a 24-inch mower, and the job would take only 120 swaths, 4.9 miles, and 1 hour and 36 minutes out of your weekend.

Whatever width you decide on, make sure the mower's height can be adjusted from at least 1 to 3 inches. Depending on the type of grass you'll be mowing, you may need to cut as low as ½ inch and as high as 4 inches.

MAKE IT EASY ON YOURSELF

There are other ways to save time besides buying a huge, wide mower. In fact, there's a lot you can do before you even roll the mower out of the garage. Consider modifying the shape of your lawn to speed up the job. The ideal shape would be an ellipse, allowing you to mow from beginning to end without ever turning. You'll probably never have an elliptical lawn, but you can approach that ideal by softening the sharp corners and dealing with obstructions.

Take a good look at your yard. You might even draw a diagram of your landscape, including the lawn, sidewalks, house, trees, shrubs, and flower beds. Mark all of the sharp corners and obstructions.

Start with the trees. Think of all the time you spend mowing around them, and then, after the mower has been put away,

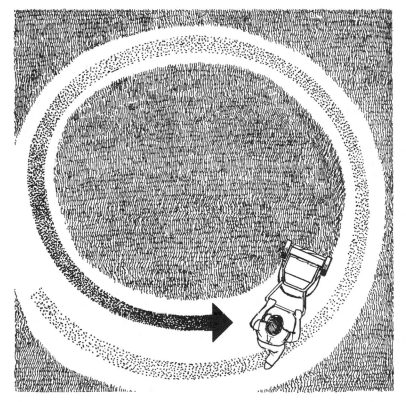

To save mowing time, cut in a circular pattern, leaving the corners unmowed until the end.

clipping around them. You can avoid much of the work by laying an attractive ring of bark mulch around the trunks, or surrounding them with a groundcover such as pachysandra or vinca. You may be able to plant groundcovers to fill in the sharp corners of your lawn, too. Do the same along your house, pathways, and gardens, and you'll be amazed at how much time you save.

You'll be doing a lot of turning no matter what shape your lawn is. But you can save time by mowing around the perimeter of the lawn rather than doing parallel rows with a 180-degree turn at each end.

And don't be afraid to cut corners — it makes good sense. Instead of mowing all the way into a corner, leave an unmowed patch there for the sake of a smoother course around the yard. After you've finished the lawn, go back and mow the corners. That little bit of time at the end will have been saved many times over during the mowing of the lawn.

If your lawnmower has its discharge chute on the right side, mow in a clockwise direction so the clippings will blow onto the unmowed area. In this way, the clippings will be cut up further by your next pass. (Occasionally, perhaps one out of four times, reverse your direction to avoid the washboard effect caused by continually mowing in one direction. This also keeps the wheels from forming ruts.) Overlap the previous swath by one-third to one-half the width of your mower.

Mowing reduces root growth and activity, and can halt root growth entirely if the mower is set too low, but you can minimize the shock by customizing your mowing techniques to meet the needs of your lawn. Keep these general rules in mind as you plan your mowing:

■ *Mow at the right height.* Some grass types are naturally low growing, and perform best when they're kept short. Letting them grow long causes thatch buildup, lets seed heads form, and spoils the lawn's appearance. Keep creeping and velvet bentgrasses cut low, about ½ inch. Colonial bentgrass, annual bluegrass, Bermuda, and zoysia should be cut at ½ to 1 inch. A medium height of 1 to 2 inches is best for buffalograss, red fescue, centipedegrass, carpetgrass, Kentucky bluegrass, perennial ryegrass, and meadow fescue. Grasses that should be kept high, between 1½ and 3 inches, include bahiagrass, tall fescue, and St. Augustinegrass.

■ *Mow lightly and frequently.* This practice will cause less stress to the grass plant. The old rule of thumb holds: Don't cut off more than a third of the grass with any one cutting. If you want to maintain your lawn at 2 inches, for example, mow before it reaches 3 inches.

■ *Mow higher and less often in the summer.* By letting the grass grow up, you allow the roots to grow down, and that means your lawn will have more staying power during times of drought. Tall grass also shades the soil to cool the plants' crowns and reduce soil drying.

■ *Mow to 1 inch higher in shady areas.* That leaves more leaf surface on the grass to increase photosynthesis and make up for light shortages.

■ *Use the right lawnmower.* Reel mowers are best for close cutting. They can't handle lawns taller than 4 inches or grasses that send up tall seed heads, such as bahiagrass and St. Augustinegrass. They also have a hard time making a clean cut on tough grasses such as ryegrass. Rotary mowers can handle high grass and weeds with ease, but won't cut evenly if set at 1 inch or lower.

The key is to treat your lawn like the living organism it is. Minimize the stress on it and you'll have a healthy lawn that's better able to resist invasion from weeds and insects. And by breaking out of an inflexible mowing schedule, you'll probably spend less time mowing. That means more time in the garden or the hammock for you.

THATCH MEETS ITS MATCH

Misunderstood, maligned, mysterious thatch. People think of thatch the same way they think about dandruff. They don't understand where it comes from, but they know it's bad. However, you shouldn't feel embarrassed by your lack of understanding. Only within the past few years have turf experts disproved the three big myths about thatch. One: Thatch is always bad in every shape and form. Two: Thatch is caused by grass clippings. Three: Thatch can be prevented by raking up those clippings after mowing.

No one is ready to promote thatch in the lawn. But the latest research shows that a little bit is not bad at all. It may even do some good. As mentioned earlier in the chapter, it returns nitrogen to a lawn. And when less than ½ inch deep, it can act as a mulch for the lawn, with all of the benefits that mulches provide, including insulating and cooling the soil and preserving moisture.

That's the good side of thatch. But if your lawn has more than ½ inch of the stuff, you're asking for trouble. A thick thatch layer is about the worst thing that can happen to your lawn. It prevents water from penetrating and serves as a breeding ground for insects. It harbors diseases, especially brown patch, dollar spot, and fusarium. By reducing the penetration of light, it forces grass to grow fast and become spindly. It prevents turf from spreading as it should. It can cause winter dieback by desiccating the grass. It leads to uneven mowing, and results in ugly brown patches on the lawn. In short, a thick layer of thatch is a sure sign that your grass system is not working correctly.

WHAT DOES IT LOOK LIKE?

One of the mysteries of thatch is its identity. Your lawn may show some scattered, dried-up grass clippings, but that's not thatch. You've got to take a close look at the turf. Any time of the year that the grass is green, grab a ruler and take a walk out to your lawn. Stroll around a bit and get a feel for the lawn under your feet. Is it firm or springy? If your feet sink deeply into the turf or your steps are especially bouncy, that's a sign of too much thatch.

Now, pick a spot somewhere out in the open, stand there, and look down. Of course you'll see the green of the grass (and maybe some weeds). And if all is well, you'll see patches of brown soil. Unless you have serious thatch, that is. Then you may not see the soil at all. Instead, there will be a tan, underlying layer of what looks like straw. Get out your ruler and check the depth of the thatch. If it's less than ¼ inch thick, there's no cause for concern. If it measures between ¼ and ½ inch, it bears watching. If it's over ½ inch thick, you should take action.

WHAT IS THATCH?

If you look closely, you may see dried grass clippings in the thatch. Some grasses, most notably bentgrass and red fescue, are thick and tough, and their clippings break down slowly. If you let your lawn grow high and mow short, the resulting mat of cuttings may lead to serious thatch.

But clippings usually aren't the main ingredient of thatch, because they typically start breaking down and providing nitrogen to the soil within a week. Instead, thatch is mainly made up of roots, stolons, and rhizomes. These plant parts are high in lignin, a fiber, and this can make them slow to decompose. Under good conditions, the lignin breaks down rapidly into humus, but a number of practices may slow the process. Ironically, most of them are on the agenda of the high-maintenance lawn, especially the indiscriminate use of chemicals: fertilizers, herbicides, insecticides, and fungicides. There are other

reasons the soil may be slow to break down thatch: overwatering, compaction, and improper mowing. But none can compare with chemicals.

In a healthy, virgin soil, the organic matter that makes up thatch is quickly decomposed by microorganisms such as bacteria, fungi, and actinomycetes, but earthworms play the most important role. Earthworms pull thatch underground, eat it, and turn out humus. If you've got a supply of earthworms in your soil, you won't have thatch. It's as simple as that. Worms' thatch-busting power has been documented. In one study, researchers "seeded" worms into a heavily thatched pasture, and two years later the thatch was completely gone.

Unfortunately for homeowners who rely on chemical lawn aids, worms and microorganisms don't take to having their environment drenched with chemicals. Gradually, the soil becomes inhospitable to them. Researchers have learned, for example, that chlorinated hydrocarbon insecticides reduce earthworm populations in the soil while increasing thatch in the turf. In one test on a Kentucky bluegrass lawn, this effect was noticed after a single annual application of the fungicides Bandane and calcium arsenate. After three years, the worms had disappeared. The grass was severely wilted in summer and thinned by drechslera leaf spot in the spring — all due to thatch buildup.

What can you do to encourage the natural thatch-busters in your soil? First, worms prefer a turf free of chemicals and acid fertilizers. They like a well-aerated, sweet soil with a pH in the range of 6.5 to 7.5, moderate amounts of nitrogen (preferably from a natural source), and plenty of organic matter. There's one good way to provide these conditions: topdressing with a substance rich in organic matter, either a rich topsoil or peat moss.

TOP-DRESSING FOR THATCH

To most lawn owners, top-dressing is a mystery. You may have heard of it as some exotic ritual performed by groundskeepers and golf course superintendents. It's certainly not akin to any practice used in vegetable or flower gardening. But it's a practice that everyone who has a lawn should know about. There's nothing difficult about it — simply cover the lawn with a thin layer of organic matter or soil. And nearly every lawn could benefit from a topdressing at least once a year.

There's a lot more to top-dressing than pleasing earthworms. It's a simple way to improve your soil base without digging up the lawn and starting over. It can improve drainage and aeration. At the same time, it buries disease spores, preventing their spread.

Top-dressing reduces thatch by speeding the natural decomposition process performed by microorganisms. If you've been applying chemicals to your lawn, you should top-dress to rescue the microorganisms. As long as the topdressing material has not been sterilized, and especially if it contains ample organic matter, it will contain microorganisms.

There are a lot of materials that can be used as top-dressing. Finely screened compost is one of the best, because it contains nutrients. In fact, top-dressing twice a year with compost will probably satisfy all of the nutritional needs of a lawn. Sand, topsoil, ground seaweed, rotted sawdust, well-rotted manure, and peat moss are other good topdressing materials.

You don't need much to do the job. Give the entire lawn a layer no thicker than 3/8 inch. Use a fertilizer spreader, or simply broadcast it by hand. About 3/4 of a cubic yard of topsoil will cover 1,000 square feet of lawn. The best time for top-dressing is the fall.

BRING YOUR LAWN TO LIFE

If getting microorganisms back into your soil is your main goal, new commercial products will do the job without the bulk and trouble of top-dressing with soil. These materials contain cultures of the microorganisms that are most effective at decomposing thatch. Researchers at the University of Michigan found that thatch was reduced by applications of Ringer's Lawn Rx (applied at 30 pounds per 1,500 square feet) and Lawn Keeper (at 25 pounds per 2,500 square feet).

In addition to introducing microorganisms, there are physical ways of cutting up and removing thatch. For moderate thatch, a good stiff raking with a wire rake will remove most of it. A cavex rake, with its wide, curved tines, will do a more thorough job. You can buy a dethatching blade for your rotary mower, but it won't be adequate for handling heavy thatch. For that, you'll need to rent or hire a verticutter or vertimower. These machines look like lawnmowers with vertical blades. They slice through the thatch and lift it to the surface where it can be raked away. A walk-behind verticutter is easy to use. It starts and operates like a lawn-mower. Make one pass over your entire lawn, then rake up the thatch and add it to your compost pile.

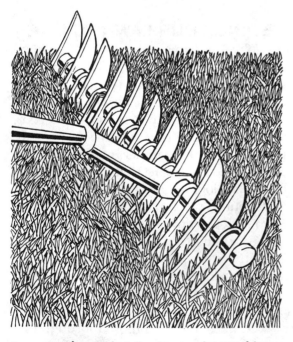

A cavex rake, or thatch rake, can be used to remove thatch from small areas.

If thatch has formed because your soil is worn out and compacted, then your problem is more serious. You can remove the thatch, but it will be back unless you improve the soil. Turf won't grow properly if the roots and microbes that live in the soil have too little oxygen. Without suffi-cient air, anaerobic respiration takes place at the roots, resulting in a potentially harm-ful buildup of carbon dioxide and ethanol. That leads to shallow root growth, a thin lawn that's vulnerable to a weed invasion, and reduced turf vigor.

In addition, compacted soils have less microbial activity. That means there's more disease, less nitrogen fixation, and an increase in thatch for most kinds of grass. Compaction of turf also increases the tem-perature at soil level. The turf can be 1° to 13°F higher in compacted soil. As a result, the turf is less vigorous. More water is needed, which will in turn increase the compaction problem.

Any kind of tillage will relieve the prob-lem to some extent by letting air into the soil. You don't have to take a plow to the whole lawn: Specialized equipment can do the job without damaging the turf. These machines poke holes in the sod to work air into the soil and break up the hard crust.

Power walk-behind aeration machines lift cores of soil from the turf. You can rent them or hire someone to do the work for you. A core cultivator is simpler and less expensive. This hand-and-foot-operated tool has handlebars and two or four hollow tines. They are available through garden supply catalogs for roughly $15. You stomp

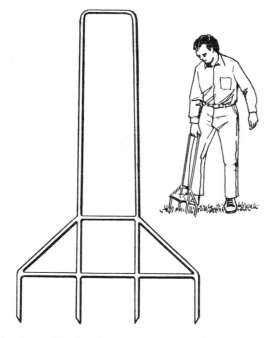

A core cultivator is an inexpensive hand tool for aerating soil and removing thatch.

the tines into the ground and then lift the handlebars to pull up cores of soil and thatch. As you move on to the next section, the cores are ejected onto the top of the

turf where they can be broken up with a rake. This leaves a layer of soil on top of the remaining thatch, which helps to break it down. It's similar to the topdressing process, and tests at the University of Illinois showed it to be as effective in removing thatch up to 1½ inches deep.

In less extreme cases, poking holes in the soil will do the trick. Gasoline-powered, tractor-mounted spikers accomplish the job quickly, but they are so heavy they will probably do more harm than good. For homeowners, the easiest way to poke holes is with a pitchfork. That's how it was done in the old days. The job will take a while, but it works for most lawns. Get yourself a sturdy pitchfork and drive it into the lawn 4 to 6 inches deep, then rock it back and forth slightly, pull it out, and repeat at equidistant intervals until you've covered the whole lawn.

Once the thatch is gone, start a program to keep it out. Stop using chemical fertilizers, insecticides, herbicides, and fungicides. Fertilize sparingly, and no more than twice a year. Take care not to overwater the lawn. Mow lightly and often. If you take care to cut off no more than a third of the grass shoots, the microorganisms will take care of the rest.

WATER WISDOM

Try to picture 27,154 gallons of water. That's a lot of H$_2$O — more than enough to fill a swimming pool 6 feet deep by 20 feet wide by 30 feet long.

Now picture yourself applying that water every week to a lawn. An actively growing 1-acre plot of grass needs that much moisture in a thorough watering. Looking at this amount of water in another way, it is a matter of 1½ to 2 inches of water per week over the entire surface. An inch or two of water may not seem like much, until you envision a layer of water that deep over the entire surface of your yard. Even a modest 5,000-square-foot lawn will consume up to 6,000 gallons per week.

But before you start toting up the water bill in your head, there are a few things to consider. You don't have to supply all of that water with a hose and a sprinkler, of course. In most of the country, a good part of it will be supplied by rain. And the soil has the capacity to store water, especially if it has been properly prepared with organic matter. Finally, those figures presuppose that you want to keep your lawn growing actively all through the summer. That may not be the case. Except in extremely dry areas, it's possible to get by without watering at all by letting the grass go dormant during the summer.

In many cases, too much water does more harm than too little. Homeowners waste a lot of time and water by trying to keep up with the Joneses, rather than responding to the lawn's real needs. Mr. Jones drags out the hose the first hot day of spring, and stands there whistling as he sprinkles his lawn. Before long, people up and down the street are following suit, unreeling hoses, setting up sprinklers, and dousing their lawns. Everyone wants to do right by their lawns, but those innocent spring sprinkles can cause serious trouble for the lawn in the summer.

PUTTING DOWN ROOTS

The more water the lawn gets early on, the more it will need later. When water is plentiful in the spring, roots get lazy. Like us, grass plants don't work any harder than they have to. They stay in the top layer of soil, where they can find plenty of water. They are not forced to drive deep, probing the subsoil for moisture. So when dry weather strikes, the roots aren't able to reach the moisture deep in the soil. And roots that sit close to the top of the soil will dry out quickly. The plants wilt, and unless they get a lot of water in a hurry, they may die.

A little water may not help at all. If you sprinkle for 10 minutes, putting on about $1/10$ inch of water, this moisture penetrates no farther than an inch and will evaporate quickly. In effect, you aren't really watering your lawn.

But if the grass is not pampered, it will be prepared for dry weather. The roots will have driven deep into the soil, searching for water in the spring, so that the grass is prepared for all but the most severe droughts without any supplemental water. In fact, you may never have to water your lawn again.

The trick is to manage your watering in a way that encourages grass to grow long, strong roots. You do that by wetting the soil to the full depth of the roots — generally 6 to 18 inches. The soil acts as a reservoir for water storage, and the more soil the roots occupy, the greater the reservoir they can tap. And this in turn extends the time between waterings.

Root depth is a function of grass species as well as your watering program. Some grasses normally dig a lot deeper than others. The bentgrasses have very shallow roots, only 1 to 8 inches long. Kentucky bluegrass, red fescue, ryegrass, St. Augustinegrass, and dichondra normally root to a depth of 8 to 18 inches. Deep-rooting grasses, those with roots that may grow as deep as 5 feet, include zoysia, bermudagrass, tall fescue, and

WHEN IN DROUGHT

Here's a rundown of the major grasses and their drought tolerance.

Drought-Tolerant	Moderately Tolerant	Drought-Susceptible
Bermudagrass	Kentucky bluegrass	Creeping bentgrass
Zoysiagrass	Canada bluegrass	Velvet bentgrass
Buffalograss	Perennial ryegrass	Colonial bentgrass
Wheat grass	St. Augustinegrass	Rough bluegrass
Tall fescue	Bahiagrass	Annual bluegrass
Fine fescue		Centipedegrass
		Annual ryegrass

crown vetch. The longer the root, the more drought-tolerant the grass.

Several other factors can affect rooting depth. Root length is directly related to the shoot height; when you mow low, you keep the roots short. Early in the spring, fertilizing and watering heavily will keep roots from stretching for nourishment.

SOIL PROFILES

It's also important to know what kind of soil is under your lawn before you drag out the hose. The soil will determine when you should water, and even which type of sprinkler you should use.

At full saturation, clay soils can hold up to 2½ inches of moisture per foot of depth; grass will be able to draw on soil moisture for up to 2½ weeks without any rain or supplemental irrigation. Loams hold 1½ inches per foot of depth. Sand will hold only ¾ of an inch. A lawn in pure sand would have no water to draw from the soil after only a week without rain.

It's best not to water until that reservoir is just about dry. Turf-care books tell you that the best time to water is just before the grass begins to wilt. They tell you how turf looks when it wilts: It turns dull, gets a grayish cast, and won't spring back after someone walks across it. But they don't tell you how grass looks *before* it starts to wilt. Here is a way to predict the wilting point. You have to know how deep the grass roots are, and how dry the soil is to that depth.

You can find that out if you do a little digging. Try this the first time you're tempted to water: Grab a spade and carry it to a normal spot in your yard, not on a hill or in a gully, not under a tree or next to a sidewalk. Dig out a block of turf the width of your spade and at least 1 foot deep. (Don't worry —you'll be able to replace the block without damaging the lawn.) Examine the soil to see how deep the roots grow. Then check the soil itself. Is it bone dry? When completely dry, heavy soils will be baked into a hard block; lighter soils will look tan and powdery. Grab a handful of soil. If it doesn't feel completely dry, the lawn doesn't need water yet. You may want to continue digging cores through the summer until you get a feel for how long it takes the soil to completely dry out.

If you take core samples around your lawn, you'll be surprised to find out how greatly the moisture content varies. Soil on top of a slope will be dry long before that at the slope's foot. Thick growths of trees or shrubs will also dry the soil. These areas may need three times as much water as the rest of the lawn. Soil in the shade dries out much more slowly than that exposed to a full day's sun. And soil that has been enriched with organic matter will hold its moisture two to three times as long as patches that are made up mostly of sand or subsoil.

HOW MUCH WATER?

When it is time to water, the soil type will dictate how much to apply and how fast to put it on. You'll want to put down a lot more water on a turf growing in clay than on one growing in sand. Two inches of water at a time is not too much for clay,

but because sand can hold only ¾ inch, any more would be wasted on it.

You can also waste water by putting it on too fast. So you should have an idea of the infiltration rate of your soil before watering. Clay, for example, absorbs water slowly. If you put it on faster than it can be absorbed, you'll waste a lot in runoff. Sand will soak up water ten times faster than clay, so you can really pour the water on and get the job done faster.

The golden rule of watering is that the flow rate of the sprinkler or hose should never exceed the infiltration rate of your soil. You'll see in the table below that the slope of the ground also influences the infiltration rate. The greater the slope, the more the runoff and the slower the infiltration.

INFILTRATION RATE OF WATER

Texture	Level (in./hr.)	45-Degree Slope (in./hr.)
Sandy	1.0	0.5
Sandy loam	0.5	0.5
Loam	0.25	0.18
Clay loam	0.15	0.1
Clay	0.1	0.08

Flow rates of sprinklers are normally printed on the packages or with the instructions. And you can easily gauge the flow rate of a hose. Get a 5-gallon bucket and a watch with a second hand. Turn the faucet on full blast and count how many seconds it takes to fill it. Divide that number by 5 for gallons per second, and divide again by 60 for gallons per minute.

What do you do if your sprinkler spits out water faster than your soil can absorb it? Cycle your watering. Don't try to water the lawn in one uninterrupted session. For example, suppose you have clay soil that will accept water at only 0.1 inch per hour and a sprinkler that puts down 0.6 inch of water per hour. Run that sprinkler straight through for 1 hour and 40 minutes, and you will have put down the required 1 inch of water. But in that time, the soil will have accepted less than 0.2 inch. The rest will be wasted.

On the other hand, if you turn the sprinkler off and on in accord with how much water the soil can accept, you won't waste a drop. Run the same sprinkler for the same amount of time, 1 hour and 40 minutes, but spread it out — 10 minutes on and 50 minutes off, and so on. That way, you'll be dispensing 0.1 inch of water per hour, exactly as much as the soil can accept. Continue that for 10 hours, and your lawn will be thoroughly watered. To figure the proper schedule for other soils and sprinklers, divide the infiltration rate (in inches per hour) by the flow rate of the sprinkler (in inches per hour). The result equals the fraction of each hour the sprinkler should be on.

SPRINKLE, SPRINKLE

Choosing a lawn sprinkler is no simple task. There are scores of models on the market. Some will put down 1 inch of water in 20 minutes, while others may take up to 16 hours to do the job. You can buy sophisticated models that are programmed to water the lawn and not the lawn furniture. The prices range from just over $1 to around $100. How do all these different types stack up against one another?

A few years ago, Rodale Press's Product Testing Department tested 16 lawn sprinkler models, representing five generic classes: fixed, impulse, oscillating, revolving, and traveling. Following test specifications set forth by the American Society of Agricultural Engineers, Rodale rated them for distribution pattern, distribution uniformity, throw radius, flow rate, and average pre-

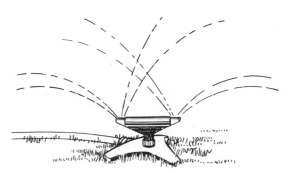

Revolving sprinklers are inexpensive, but they don't cover much ground, and the coverage from their revolving arms is not very uniform.

cipitation rate. The results were extrapolated to give average figures for precipitation rate in inches per hour and the amount of time it takes each sprinkler to put down 1 inch of water.

Revolving sprinklers are generally the least costly. They operate by shooting water out of two or three arms which are spun around by water pressure. Of the five models tested, the maximum coverage radius ranged from 10 to 20 feet. Though no type of sprinkler provided uniform coverage along the radius, the revolving types were perhaps the worst. Most dropped heavy accumulations of water near the base. On average, 90 percent of the water fell from 6 to 16 feet of the base.

Fixed sprinklers shoot water through a pattern of holes in their heads. Many of them offer the advantage of different heads

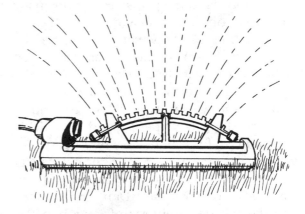

Oscillating sprinklers spread water over large rectangular patterns. Be sure to buy a quality model that doesn't puddle water at the farthest reach of its throw.

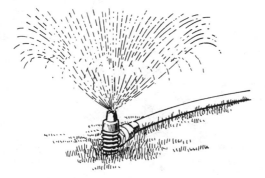

Fixed sprinklers shoot water through a pattern of holes in their heads, but they tend to leak.

on one sprinkler, so that you can dial a pattern of choice: circle, square, fan, semicircle, and so on. This type seemed to be the leakiest and to cover the least ground, although coverage varied according to pattern.

Oscillating sprinklers cover a rectangular pattern as their tube rocks back and forth. Many can be programmed to water only one side. This type is often plagued by unevenness of water distribution, leaving puddles near the end of the arcs as the sprinkler pauses before reversing itself.

Impulse sprinklers shoot water out in a jet which is broken into small drops by an adjustable diffuser pin. The force of the water also turns the sprinkler head. Some models have adjustable ranges and patterns. In general, the impulse sprinklers in the test demonstrated the greatest range and uniformity, although they did leave a fairly heavy accumulation near the base.

Traveling sprinklers have arms like revolving sprinklers, but the bases travel along the lawn, dragging the hose behind them. Both of the models tested had a low precipitation rate.

What qualities are most important in a lawn sprinkler? Naturally, sprinklers with the greatest throw length have to be moved less frequently. Sprinklers with a high precipitation rate don't have to spend as much time in one place to get the job done; they're best for sandy soils, but they waste water on clay soils that have a slow infiltration rate. For clay, look for a sprinkler with a low precipitation rate.

Generally, there's a trade-off between precipitation rate and throw length. Fixed sprinklers generally have a high precipita-

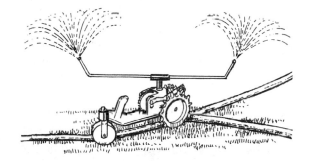

Traveling sprinklers have arms like revolving sprinklers, but the entire housing moves across the lawn to provide superior coverage.

tion rate, for example, but don't cover much ground. That information should be on the package. If it's not, ask for it.

Uniformity may be the most important quality when it comes to the well-being of the lawn. Puddles and dry patches lead to uneven growth, and can give rise to diseases and insects. To avoid uneven turf growth, don't place the sprinkler in the same spot time after time. Make sure couplings are tight, and check for leaks periodically. When possible, operate the sprinklers at full pressure to reduce loss through evaporation.

WATER ON DEMAND

A watering schedule doesn't have to be complicated, especially if you live in the North. South of the bluegrass line, however, it may be necessary to keep watering carefully during the hot summer weather. Bermudagrass is able to go a long time

Impulse sprinklers are modeled after the type commonly used on farms. They have good range and uniformity.

without water, but it must have some. Blue gramagrass will survive a dry summer, although it will turn completely brown, but it cannot be grown in the hottest areas. The same is true of buffalograss. St. Augustinegrass is shallow-rooted like bentgrass, so it must be watered often. Many California lawns are Kentucky bluegrass, and they must be watered every week in the summer.

Northern lawns seldom die of thirst even if they are not watered at all, provided they are planted in good soil containing plenty of organic matter and are mowed properly. The exception is bentgrass, which is very shallow-rooted and has no business in a low-maintenance lawn anyway.

Northern grasses handle the heat and dryness of summer by going semi-dormant. As the days grow longer, the temperature rises and water is less available, so the grass grows more slowly. If the weather is hot and dry enough, a lawn begins to turn brown. That scares people. But if you don't mind facing the color for a few weeks, the grass will snap back as summer draws to a close and temperatures moderate.

More watering means more mowing and more chance of disease. And heavy fertilization means more watering. Studies have shown that lawns fertilized every month during the summer require 13 percent more water than those fertilized only once.

If your lawn shows serious signs of wilt—a dull gray color, a lack of springiness so that footprints remain in the grass after you walk over it—water may be called for. And that means a thorough drenching. (There are only two times when light watering is called for: on newly seeded lawns, and to cool the grass and prevent diseases during extreme heat waves.)

You may have heard that watering during the heat of the day will scald the grass. That's not true. But it is the least efficient time to water, because the heat speeds evaporation of the water so that less will get to the roots.

There's also a common warning against watering at night. The reasoning is that the water will sit all night on the grass without evaporating and thus encourage disease. The current theory, however, is that the grass will probably be wet from dew during the night anyway. Watering in the morning or early evening would keep it wet even longer, giving diseases more time to take hold. So, water after the dew has dried or during the afternoon; water only if there's need; and, when you water, water enough.

7

CHEMICAL-FREE WEED WARFARE

Weedy lawns are apt to frustrate organic gardeners, expecially if they believe the propaganda spread by chemical companies — that you have to either use herbicides or settle for a weedy lawn.

But this is just not true. Good lawns have been around a lot longer than herbicides. And lawns have a better chance of being good when they're not subjected to these chemicals. You *can* have a good-looking, virtually weedless lawn without resorting to dangerous and expensive chemicals. But first, you have to be aware of the laws of the lawn.

WEEDY IS IN THE EYE OF THE BEHOLDER

What is a weed? That's a matter of how you think a lawn should look. If you want your backyard to resemble a golf green, then everything but bentgrass is a weed. But if you're looking for a pretty place to play ball with the kids or have a barbecue, then you can afford to stretch the definition of what is acceptable.

Society's perception of weeds has changed over the years, and so has the roster of the worst weeds. A flower today might be a weed tomorrow, and vice versa.

Take clover — please. Not too long ago, a clover lawn was a sign of prestige. The silky green leaves and pastel flowers made delightful lawns, though not well-suited for heavy traffic. Clover is soft to walk on. It mows well, looks good, and smothers other so-called weeds. Clover seed was sold by the bushelful to estates, or mixed with grass seed for thick combination lawns. Until the 1950s, clover was as common in a home lawn mix as bluegrass. Then a major producer of grass seed and chemicals launched a public relations campaign disparaging clover. Clover is a weed, the company declared. It doesn't belong in the modern lawn. Not so coincidentally, this same company introduced a chemical to kill clover. Its point of view carried the day, and now homeowners spend a lot of time and money trying to get rid of this once-popular plant, blind to its fine qualities.

What about dandelions? Are they weeds? Not to the kid making dandelion

Clover was once a common and highly valued lawn plant, but today it is considered a weed.

chains or blowing puffballs. Not to the grandpa making dandelion wine. And not to the farmers of Vineland, New Jersey, who grow dandelions in neat rows as a cash crop. The tasty greens are harvested and sold fresh in markets up and down the East Coast, and are also sent to canneries and supermarkets. On those Vineland dandelion farms, *turfgrass* is the weed, and it is diligently eradicated from the dandelion fields.

Ask yourself if you can stand a few dandelions in the lawn. What harm are they doing? They might not make it on a baseball field where a bad hop can mean the difference between a win and a loss, but they're not likely to ruin a picnic.

Many of the weeds you'll find listed later in this chapter were intentionally introduced to this country as groundcovers. Some, like veronica and violets, are still listed in wildflower books and are even featured in nursery catalogs. Other weeds are perfectly fine grasses that happen to be growing out of place. Bentgrass and tall fescue are considered weeds if found in a pure Kentucky bluegrass lawn.

If you make up your mind that they're not weeds, you won't have to get rid of them. Of course, there are some weeds that can't possibly pass for anything else. Plantain, with its ugly seed heads towering over the grass on scrawny stalks, has got to go. That's a weed, pure and simple.   And if your lawn is less than 25 percent grass, you've got a real weed problem that must be dealt with.

It's up to you to decide how many weeds you can stand, and which ones absolutely have to go. But don't try to get rid of all of them at once. Pick the one that makes your skin crawl and your teeth grind and go after that. Get rid of it by pulling, mowing, or cutting, and then follow the cultural steps for keeping it out.

If you have just a few weeds, pull, dig, or cut them. If you have an infestation — more than 25 percent of your lawn is one particular weed — use the appropriate cultural methods, but keep an eye on the lawn. A method such as low mowing might cure one weed problem only to give rise to another. If that happens, you'll have to nip it in the bud.

The best defense against weeds is a healthy lawn. If the lawn is thick and vigorous, there won't be room for weeds to elbow their way in. A lawn that's fertilized properly will start up early in the spring before cool-season weeds can germinate. A lawn that's watered correctly will resist summer stress at the time when warm-season weeds are gearing up. Mowing the right way will both encourage thick grass growth and shade emerging weeds. Out in the lawn jungle, it's survival of the fittest. If the lawn is healthy, the weeds won't stand a chance.

THERE'S NO SUCH THING AS A QUICK FIX

If you start with a weedy lawn, good grass care will eventually force weeds out, but this takes time. You can help the process along by expending a little elbow grease in pulling, chopping, digging, and cutting weeds. And if you know when to intervene and have the right tools, it's easier than you might think. Maybe not quite as easy as zapping the lawn with poison, but far better for the lawn — and you.

There are plenty of reasons to avoid herbicides. Even if you don't care about their effect on your family's health, think about what they're doing to the lawn.

Weeds are symptoms of problems. They are signs that the lawn is in distress. The good thing about weeds is that, for the most part, they don't like good growing conditions. They're survivors that thrive under conditions that other plants shy away from. They'll grow in spots that grass can't handle — shady spots, sites with compacted soil, underfertilized plots, and areas that are too wet or too dry. Herbicides may kill off those weeds, but they don't do anything to correct the problem. Unless those conditions are changed, the weeds will return, requiring more and more herbicides.

Herbicides are poisons. In addition to killing weeds, they slow down the biological activity of the soil. This weakens grass plants, fosters thatch, and encourages diseases. Your lawn is better off without them, according to Sheila Daar. She is a landscape contractor, editor of *Common Sense Pest Control Quarterly*, and consultant to parks, athletic fields, and municipalities. "It's very standard practice to use methods where chemicals aren't required," she says. "There's nothing exotic about it. You just have to do what the textbooks tell you."

Weeds in the lawn result from any of several bad management practices, Daar explains. If you can discover the reasons and eliminate them, the weeds suddenly become manageable.

One of the main causes of weed infestation is growing the wrong type of grass. "Kentucky bluegrass is a poor choice for most areas," Daar says, "though it's still one of the most popular varieties. But it won't grow well under problem conditions. It's thin, leaving bare ground for weeds to take root. The homeowner would be better off choosing another type that does well under shady conditions, or can stand heavy traffic or light water."

Other conditions that weeds love include heavy use, soil compaction, improper fertilization, drought, and mowing too closely, especially during dormant season.

Even under perfect conditions, there still may be a few weeds, Sheila Daar admits. "But they are easy to pull out by hand."

A weed strategy should include several tactics: pulling and digging weeds; mowing, watering, and fertilizing correctly; analyzing the problem and recognizing the enemy; improving soil; topdressing; reseeding; shading; and sterilizing. It may take only one of these techniques to make your lawn presentable. It may take more. But you *can* rid a lawn of weeds without chemicals.

THE LAWN IS A GARDEN OF GRASS

Thinking of your lawn as a garden can take the mystery out of weed eradication. In your vegetable or flower garden, you take good care of the soil and you fertilize the plants. And weeds? You probably pull or hoe them. Why not do the same for your lawn? It doesn't have to mean a lot of time on your knees if you have the right tools.

THE BAD GUYS OUTNUMBER THE GOOD GUYS

It helps to keep in mind the sheer number of weed seeds around. A typical acre contains more than 200 million weed seeds in the top 6 inches of soil; that's more than 5,000 per square foot. Whenever soil is cultivated, turned over, or left bare, you can expect about 5 percent of those seeds to germinate—or about 250 growing weeds for every square foot of soil. If you sow lawn seed at the recommended rate, the viable weed seeds would outnumber the grass seeds by about two to one. (On top of that, grass seed may contain up to 5 percent weed seed.)

Whenever you pull or dig a weed, there are plenty more waiting to replace it. You have to beat them to the punch by filling in the bare patch with lawn. You should always have a small supply of grass seed on hand for reseeding. But *resodding* will fill in the spot faster. Because sod is expensive and difficult to store, you might want to plant your own sod nursery. Pick a spot on the edge of the lawn or garden, maybe 3 feet by 5 feet. It would be a good idea to enclose it with an edging. Then sow the species of your lawn grass in the bed. Whenever you

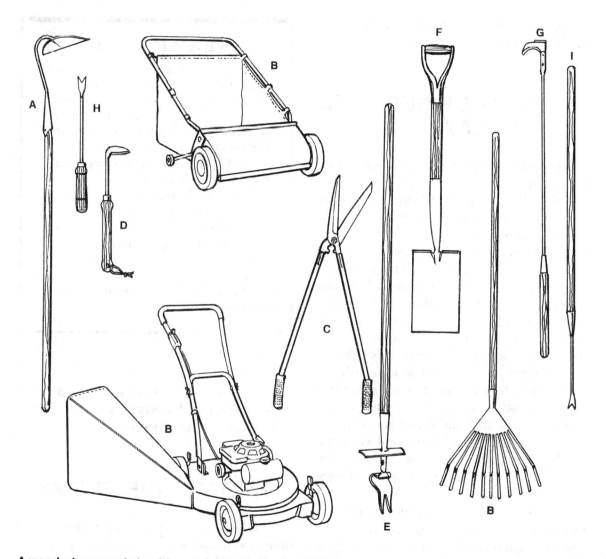

A weeder's arsenal should contain several tools: *(A)* A hoe for chopping weeds in bare areas; *(B)* a lawn sweeper, rake, or bagging attachment for sweeping up weed clippings when they are in seed; *(C)* long-handled clippers for chopping annual and perennial weeds; *(D)* a long-handled weed knife or spudd (a sharp tool with a twisted head) for cutting and digging roots of perennial weeds; *(E)* a weed popper for pulling roots of perennial weeds; *(F)* a spade for digging and splitting clumps of weed grasses; *(G)* a briar hook for pulling large weeds without bending; (H) an asparagus knife for cutting off taproots of perennial weeds; and *(I)* a long-handled version of the asparagus knife, sometimes called a dandelion digger.

dig up a clump of weeds from the lawn, dig a clump of home-grown sod to replace it.

STARTING A WEED-FREE LAWN

If you want to establish a lawn in an especially weedy area, try an old farming practice known as fallowing. It simply involves leaving the area bare for a time before planting your crop—in this case, grass. If you're planning to sow a lawn in fall, till the patch in early to midsummer. Shortly after the ground is turned, annual weeds will germinate and perennial weeds will sprout. Plow or till again to turn them under. A second crop will appear. Turn them under as well. In the process, you're forcing dormant weed seeds to germinate, then killing them, and bringing perennial weed roots and stolons to the surface, where many dry out and die. If you like, you can rake out grassy weed roots and runners. Finally, till again just before sowing the grass so that you don't give weeds a chance to get a head start.

There's a modern practice that also forces weeds to grow and die. It's called soil solarization, and it requires only a sheet of clear plastic and hot, sunny weather. About a month before sowing, water the ground deeply, then spread one layer of clear plastic tightly over the area, holding down the edges with boards or plenty of soil. Weeds will germinate rapidly, and then the intense heat under the plastic will fry

---

WEED-BUSTING

1. Prepare the soil by correcting compaction and drainage problems, and by adding organic matter and organic fertilizers.

2. Don't try to put a lawn where grass won't grow; pave traffic areas and paths, and plant groundcovers in heavy shade.

3. Choose the right grass species and variety for your conditions.

4. Buy good, weed-free seed.

5. Sow at the right time (fall in the North, spring in the South).

6. Water thoroughly until the grass germinates.

7. Take special steps before sowing weedy areas (see Starting a Weed-Free Lawn on this page).

---

them. By the time you're ready to sow, most of the weed seeds in the upper layer of the soil will have been killed.

KNOW THINE ENEMY

There are more weeds in this world than just about anything else, except maybe bugs. But they can be classified according to several categories. The weeds in your lawn may be grassy or broadleaf; annual, biennial, or perennial; and cool-season or warm-season. And they come in just about every combination. There are annual warm-season broadleaf weeds; annual cool-season grassy weeds; perennial cool-season grassy weeds; and on and on. The categories into which they fall suggest how to control them.

Grassy weeds are species of grasses, sometimes very similar to the grasses you're cultivating in your lawn. They are difficult to control because they often prefer the same conditions as lawn grasses. Grassy weeds can be bunching or spreading; annual, biennial, or perennial; and warm- or cool-season.

Broadleaf weeds are best defined by what they're not. This group includes everything that's not a grass. The leaves are not necessarily broad. Like the grassy weeds, they can be upright or creeping; annual, biennial, or perennial; and warm- or cool-season.

Annual weeds are plants that complete their life cycle in one year: They germinate from seed, grow, set seed, and die. Once they're gone, they're gone. But they leave seeds to carry on. A single plant may produce tens or even hundreds of thousands of seeds if allowed to grow. This means you'll have a population explosion the following year. There are grassy, broadleaf, warm-season, and cool-season annuals.

Biennial weeds complete their lifespans in two years. They usually spend their first year growing and their second year flowering and setting seed. They are included with perennial weeds in the listing on page 122.

Perennial weeds can spread vegetatively (by spreading roots and stems) or by seed. They can live and spread for several years.

Cool-season weeds germinate or sprout in spring or fall. Fall-germinating weeds, even annual ones, may winter over and resume growth in the spring. They grow most vigorously in spring and fall in the North and during the winter in the South. They may die or go dormant during the summer.

Warm-season weeds germinate in late spring or summer and grow actively during hot weather. They will die or go dormant during the cool weather of the winter.

WHAT WEEDS WANT

Weeds aren't fussy. They just want a comfortable place with plenty of food, water, and sunlight, where they can live, raise a family — and eventually take over the world. Give them what they want and they'll never leave. To get rid of them, you've got to know what they want and make sure they don't get it. Haphazard mowing, watering, and fertilizing can lead to trouble. Conversely, doing these common lawn practices right can be your best weed-fighting techniques.

High mowing will shade low-growing weeds and the seeds of dormant pest plants to keep them from developing. Studies at the University of Maryland show the remarkable effects of high mowing on weed populations. Researchers counted the weeds per 100 square feet in two patches of lawn. One was mowed at 1½ inches, the other at 2½ inches. After the first year, there were 15 weeds in the low-mowed areas, and only 1 in the high-mowed area. After two years, there were 53 weeds in the low-mowed patch, and only 8 in the high-mowed plot.

Frequent mowing may discourage some weeds by cutting off flowers, seed heads, and growth points. But short grass allows plenty of light to reach weed seeds, encouraging them to germinate.

In the spring, cool-season weed seeds are raring to go. A dose of quick-acting, soluble nitrogen is just what they need to begin a healthy life. Of course young grass is also hungry after a long winter. But it has reserves if it was fertilized the fall before. On the other hand, warm-season weeds want fertilizer in summer. Grass that has been fertilized earlier will be vigorous enough to withstand an invasion by them.

The same goes for water. Cool-season weeds thrive on frequent light sprinklings in spring and fall; warm-season weeds want the same in summer. To thwart them, water lawns only when necessary. Deep, infrequent watering *before* stress sets in will help your grass develop deep roots and an ability to withstand drought.

As you can see, weed control isn't all cut and dried. A cultural practice that will foil one weed might please another. The control of weeds depends on the categories they belong to. You have to understand the difference between the needs of the weeds and those of your grass. But before you can do that, you have to have a working familiarity with the modus operandi of the weeds. The following rogue's gallery of

weeds offers a look at the most common lawn spoilers, with general control recommendations for categories and specific advice for each type. The information below tells how to control cool-season weeds; this section is followed by tips on handling warm-season lawn invaders.

COOL-SEASON WEEDS

Cool-season weeds are a problem in actively growing northern lawns and in dormant southern lawns. They're vigorous early in the spring when warm-season grasses are still lethargic from the winter, and again in the fall when the grasses are slowing down. In the winter, they invade a dormant warm-season lawn and make a mess of it. In the South, the best way to beat them to the punch is to plant a winter grass. Overseed a cool-season turfgrass like Kentucky bluegrass or perennial ryegrass.

Remove as many of the weeds as possible before they have a chance to set seed. For small problems, you can pull or cut the weeds. Mowing may be enough to control them, but when you have a serious infestation, it will help to rake up the clippings.

COOL-SEASON ANNUALS

Pull, cut, or hoe these weeds before their flowers and seeds appear. Fertilize turf in the fall. In the North, mow high in the spring and fall. In the South, mow high in late summer and plant a winter grass in fall.

Cool-season annuals germinate early in the spring and late in the fall, when the

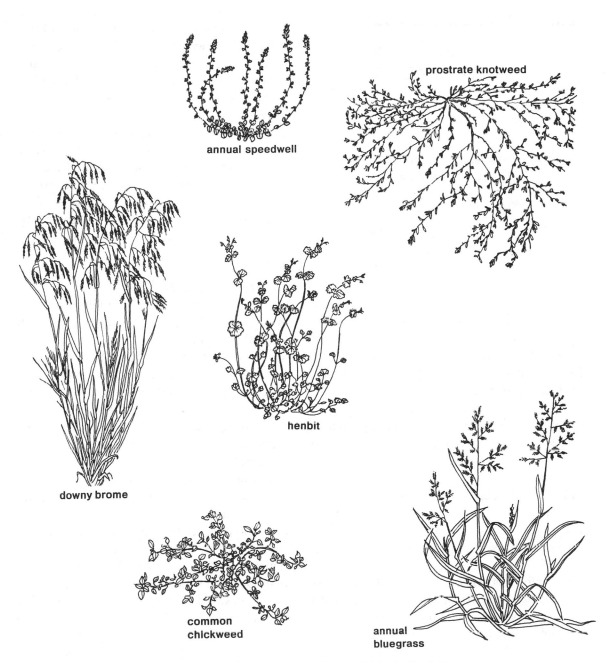

annual speedwell

prostrate knotweed

downy brome

henbit

common chickweed

annual bluegrass

Cool-season annual weeds germinate early in the spring and late in the fall.

COOL-SEASON ANNUAL WEEDS

Weed Grasses	Broadleaf Weeds
Annual bluegrass	Black medic
Downy bromegrass	Common chickweed
	Henbit
	Mallow
	Prostrate knotweed
	Speedwell
	Violets

and compacted moist soil that is frequently irrigated. It needs strong light for germination. Control by raising the mower and mowing more often. Remove clippings when seed heads are present, and dig out clumps of weed.

Downy bromegrass (*Bromus tectorum*) is slender and erect, with coarse leaves. It is common in fall-seeded turf, and occurs throughout the United States, except in the extreme Southeast. It plagues thin, neglected turf and cool soils. Control by hand weeding.

BROADLEAF WEEDS

Common chickweed (*Stellaria media*) is a ground-hugging annual with small smooth, oblong, pointed leaves. It bears small, individual white flowers that bloom throughout the growing season, and sets seed any time after flowering. Seeds germinate from late fall to early spring. Roots grow from the stem nodes to form new plants. Common chickweed occurs throughout the United States in poorly drained or shady areas. It likes frequent light watering. Control by cutting or pulling, beginning early in the spring. Rake up stems, because immature seed will continue to mature and spread after the parent plant dies. Maintain vigorous turf. Water infrequently but deeply when chickweed is present.

Prostrate knotweed (*Polygonum aviculare*) appears in early spring, forming circular mats of slender, wiry stems with smooth, bluish-green leaves and very small white flowers. Stems do not root. Knotweed

soil temperature is under 60°F. To slow their germination and spread, make sure the lawn is not receiving water and fertilizer at those times. Keep the grass mowed high in the spring and fall to shade the soil and discourage germination.

In general, make sure that the lawn is thick and that there are no open spaces for weeds to take hold—they will if given the chance.

WEED GRASSES

Annual bluegrass (*Poa annua*) is a light green, low-growing, bunch-type relative of Kentucky bluegrass. It is classified as a weed because it goes to seed early and browns out during hot summers. Annual bluegrass produces seed throughout the growing season, especially in spring. It occurs mainly in cool, humid areas, but will grow wherever Kentucky bluegrass does. It likes mild temperatures (with the soil 60° to 70°F) germinates in mid- to late winter and appears throughout the United States, especially in cool climates. It favors compacted soils, such as heavily traveled areas along sidewalks and driveways. Control by pulling or cutting in summer; aerate soil in heavily trafficked areas.

Black medic (*Medicago lupulina*) is a legume with foliage that resembles white clover. Though an annual, it is sometimes as long-lived as a perennial. It appears in late spring or summer and sends out bright yellow flowers. Black medic is common throughout the United States, and shows up in dry, high-phosphorus soils. Control it by pulling or digging the shallow taproot, and by watering turf deeply as needed in early summer.

Henbit (*Lamium amplexicaule*), as a member of the mint family, has a square stem and rounded, coarse leaves. Flowers are trumpet-shaped and pale purple. Seeds mature April to June, germinating in early fall or sometimes in early spring. It takes to moist, fertile soil and thin or new turf. Because it is shallow-rooted, pulling works well as a control; because it grows low, mowing does not. Henbit is troublesome in lawns newly seeded in late summer and fall. So, when establishing a new lawn in a henbit-infested area, leave the ground bare through late summer, till regularly to kill newly emerging seedlings before they set seed, and sow turfgrass in the fall.

Speedwells (*Veronica* spp.) are creeping weeds that occur mainly in cool, humid regions. Some species are annual, while others are perennial. Leaves are usually small and lobed; flowers are blue to purple with white throats. Seedpods resemble hearts. Seeds germinate in the spring. Speedwells like cool, moist soils and thin turf. Because they creep and root at the nodes, they are difficult to pull, and hoeing works better. Treat them as a cool-season weed. Fertilize the lawn in fall so that it starts growing vigorously in spring before speedwell can germinate. Mow high in spring.

Mallow (*Malva neglecta*) develops a thick taproot from which non-rooting stems emerge. The leaves are round and hairy. White to lilac flowers appear from May through summer. It's found throughout the United States, especially in cool areas on fertile soils and on stressed turf. Pull the weeds early in summer, and use a low-fertility schedule.

Violets (*Viola* spp.) are marked by their broad, round, or heart-shaped leaves and of course by their delicate pink, white, yellow, or purple flowers. They like shade and cool, moist, fertile soils. If you really *must* rid your lawn of these flowers, mow low, improve drainage, reduce irrigation, and aerate.

COOL-SEASON PERENNIALS

Creeping perennial broadleaf weeds are among the toughest to handle. Because they hug the ground and root at the nodes, they're hard to get at and chop or pull. The best way to remove them is by raking vigorously early in the season and putting them in leaf bags. Then mow at the short end of the recommended length for your grass, and remove the clippings. Fertilize the lawn in the fall after frost to get it off to a vigorous start in the spring. In extreme cases, you may have to aerate the turf in the spring, or correct problem areas with drain tiles or by adding organic matter.

WEED GRASSES

These are tough to handle because they are so closely related to the grasses that are growing in your lawn. In fact, some of them may be exactly what your neighbor seeded. For example, bentgrass is a highly prized grass as a putting green, but it's a weed if you find it growing in patches in your bluegrass lawn. Tall fescue is a weed in a bentgrass lawn, just as bentgrass is a weed in a tall fescue lawn.

The best bet is to dig out the foreign grass and replace it immediately with your favored species. You can also pull or dig the unwanted grass before seed heads form in fall. Fertilize in late fall. In both spring and fall, don't water unless absolutely necessary. Mow high in spring and fall to shade the grass and slow germination.

Wild garlic (*Allium vineale*) and **wild onion** (*A. canadense*) are not actually grasses. They may be the first green you see in the spring, growing in tufts in the spring lawn. The slender, hollow stems give off an odor of garlic or onions when cut. They grow from small bulbs produced underground, and favor cool temperatures and thin turf. You can control them by mowing low; the turf won't be damaged, because the grass hasn't even greened up yet. This will remove the previous year's brown tips. But unless the underground bulbs are dug up, the plants will sprout again.

Smooth bromegrass (*Bromus inermis*) has gray-green to blue-green leaves. It spreads by rhizomes. This weed appears very early in the spring; growth slows during the summer, but plants are reinvigorated in the fall. It is found in thin, open, undernourished, infrequently mowed turf. To control it, mow low and frequently, fertilize in the fall, and water when necessary.

Timothy (*Pheleum pratense*) is a blue-green bunch grass that grows most actively in spring and fall. The leaves are broad and pointed. It frequently occurs in newly seeded areas that were once pasture, and thrives in thin, undernourished turf. Dig up clumps, and reseed with turf.

Tall fescue (*Festuca arundianacea*) is a common pasture and lawn grass charac-

---

COOL-SEASON PERENNIAL WEEDS

Weed Grasses	Broadleaf Weeds
Bentgrass	Broadleaf plantain
Quack grass	Canada thistle
Smooth bromegrass	Creeping bellflower
Tall fescue	Dandelion
Timothy	Ground ivy
Wild garlic	Mouseear chickweed
Wild onion	Speedwell
	Violets
	White clover

terized by its bunchlike growth and broad leaves. It likes dry soil and underfertilized turf. Control as for timothy.

Quack grass (*Agropyron repens*) is light green to blue-green in color. It spreads by large, white rhizomes in spring and fall, and does best in cool temperatures. To check it, mow low, then pull or cut and remove the runners; or slice the plants with a spade in summer.

Bentgrass (*Agrostis palustris*) is another common lawn grass, used primarily for high-maintenance turf such as golf greens. As a weed, it spoils turf by forming patches of low-growing, fine-leaved grass. It likes cool temperatures, frequent watering, and low mowing. Control it by digging out clumps and reseeding. Mow high, and do not water unless necessary.

BROADLEAF WEEDS

White clover (*Trifolium repens*) is distinguished by its three-part, emerald green leaves with white crescent markings and its white to pink flowers. It is a vigorous creeper, and does its best on thin, undernourished turf with abundant moisture. Control by pulling or cutting in spring. Keep soil phosphorus low.

Ground ivy (*Glechoma hederacea*) has the square stems characteristic of the mint family. Look also for round leaves and lavender trumpet-shaped flowers that bloom early in the spring. Ground ivy was introduced originally as a groundcover. It reproduces by seed and creeping stems, and grows in either sun or shade as long as the soil is poorly drained. Control it in spring by raising the runners with a stiff raking and by mowing close.

Mouseear chickweed (*Cerastium vulgatum*) has small white flowers that appear in late spring and early summer. The seeds mature in midsummer. Stems are low and spreading, and they root at the nodes. Leaves are fleshy and fuzzy. This chickweed likes shade and soils that are moist and poorly drained. To control, rake it vigorously in spring to raise the runners and stems, then mow close and collect the clippings to remove the runners.

Speedwells (*Veronica* spp.) are small, creeping plants with narrow leaves and smooth, rooting stems. Flowers are white to blue, and form heart-shaped seedpods. Seeds begin to germinate in the spring. Speedwell thrives in cool, moist soils and thin turf. Control as for mouseear chickweed, above.

Canada thistle (*Cirsium arvense*) is known by its ground-hugging, spiky rosette of leaves. It spreads rapidly from a long taproot. It is found in thin, undernourished turf. Pull the weeds with a weed popper or a spudd (a long-bladed knife with a 90-degree twist at the point), removing as much taproot as possible. Fertilize the area and reseed.

Broadleaf plantain (*Plantago rugelii*) has wide, oval leaves that grow in a rosette from the central stem. Seed heads rise high above the leaves on tall, narrow stems. This weed likes thin, poorly fertilized turf. Control by digging and disposing of the plant; or mow to cut stems and seed heads, then remove them.

(continued on page 126)

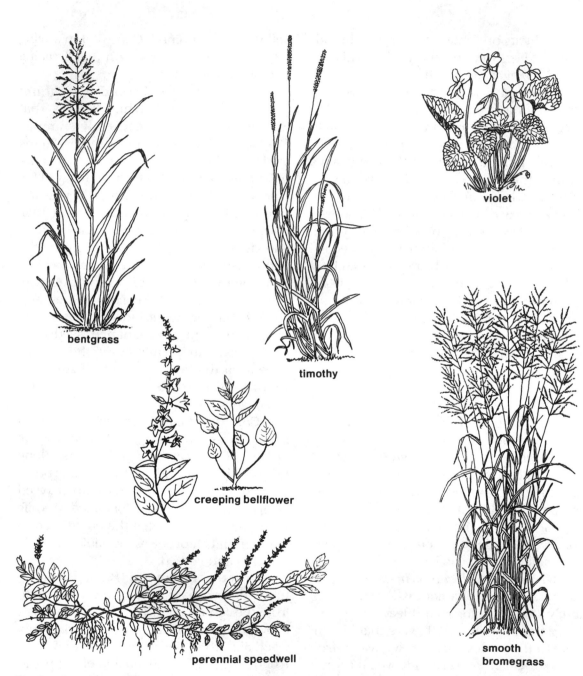

bentgrass

timothy

violet

creeping bellflower

smooth
bromegrass

perennial speedwell

Cool-season perennial weeds, shown above and on facing page, may show the first green on your lawn in spring.

mouseear chickweed

quack grass

wild garlic

tall fescue

ground ivy

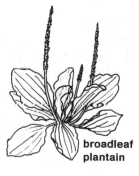

broadleaf
plantain

Creeping bellflower (*Campanula rapunculoides*) may sometimes be mistaken for a violet. The bottom leaves are heart-shaped; the top leaves on the 3-foot stem are smaller. The flowers are purple and bell-shaped. Creeping bellflower is found throughout cool humid regions, and it prefers cool temperatures and fertile soil. To control, dig bellflowers out by the root, and transplant them to your perennial flower garden.

Dandelion (*Taraxacum officinale*) needs no introduction. The bright yellow flowers, blooming primarily in spring but sporadically throughout the season, are followed by puffball seed heads. The plant may also spread from its long taproot. Seedlings germinate throughout the season. Dandelions like thin turf. To control them, pull or cut as much of the taproot as possible, and mow and remove clippings when seed heads are present. For more methods, see the box, Two Ways to Beat Dandelions, on page 127.

WARM-SEASON WEEDS

Warm-season weeds are classified just like their cool-season cousins, but because their growth cycles are different, you have to use different strategies to control them. Learn to recognize these warm-weather weeds so you can get rid of them —permanently—and get on with the lawn.

WARM-SEASON ANNUALS

These weeds are especially troublesome in the North. Their peak activity is in

---

WARM-SEASON ANNUAL WEEDS

Weed Grasses	Broadleaf Weeds
Barnyard grass	Common purslane
Crabgrass	Prostrate spurge
Foxtail	Puncture vine
Goose grass	Spotted spurge
Sandbur	Yellow woodsorrel
Stink grass	
Witchgrass	

---

the dead of summer, when cool-season grasses are stressed or dormant from the heat. In the South, they are favored by lawn pampering, summer watering, and fertilization. They germinate when the soil temperature is 60° to 65°F.

To control warm-season annuals, mow at the recommended height and remove clippings when seed heads are present; avoid summer fertilization, water only when necessary, and aerate the soil to reduce compaction.

WEED GRASSES

Warm-season annual grasses are usually favored by close mowing, summer fertilization, and light watering. They are apt to show up in turf that has been thinned by such factors as traffic or disease. You can aerate the soil to reduce compaction, and cut or pull the weeds before they can set seed.

Barnyard grass (*Echinochloa crusgalli*) is a low-growing, shallow-rooted, red to purple weed that appears in the late summer and fall throughout the United States, except in the extreme Southeast. It likes good light, adequate moisture, thin turf, close mowing, summer fertilization, and light, frequent watering. To control it, cut, hoe, or pull

from spring to summer; water turf only when necessary; and mow high.

Goose grass (*Elusine indica*) resembles crabgrass but is darker in color, with a silver center. Although it is a spreading grass, it does not root at the nodes. It germinates several weeks after crabgrass in late spring and early summer, with a soil temperature of 60° to 65°F. Goose grass likes compacted and poorly drained soils,

(continued on page 130)

TWO WAYS TO BEAT DANDELIONS

Get yourself long-handled clippers, a long-handled weed fork, or a weed popper, and go after them with the confidence that you're really accomplishing something.

One of the biggest lawn hoaxes foisted on an unsuspecting public by the chemical companies is that you can't kill dandelions without herbicides. Of course you can! You can't kill them as quickly, but you can kill them just as dead. In fact, you can clean just about every dandelion out of your lawn in one year.

It is true that dandelions are painfully persistent. Their long taproots are hard to pull, and small pieces left behind will regenerate into new weeds. But they're not indestructible. You can wear them down. The key is to get to them when they're at their weakest. That's when they're blooming, and when food reserves in the roots are at their lowest. Dig out 4 to 5 inches of the root, and you have better than an 80 percent chance that any remaining root

pieces won't have enough strength to send up another stalk. Researchers have had total success with this method.

That may mean a lot of digging and crawling around on your hands and knees. But there are tools that can make the job easier. A weed popper pulls out the plants, roots and all, with a stomp. A long-handled weeding fork lets you do the job while standing.

Cutting with long-handled shears is even easier, although one cut won't do it. You have to cut off all the leaves and as much of the stem as possible—that's lower than a lawnmower will reach—and you have to do it five or six times a year. The root will keep sending up new growth until it runs out of steam (providing you're not keeping it well supplied with fertilizer between cuttings). In one study, 92 percent of the dandelions were killed by this method.

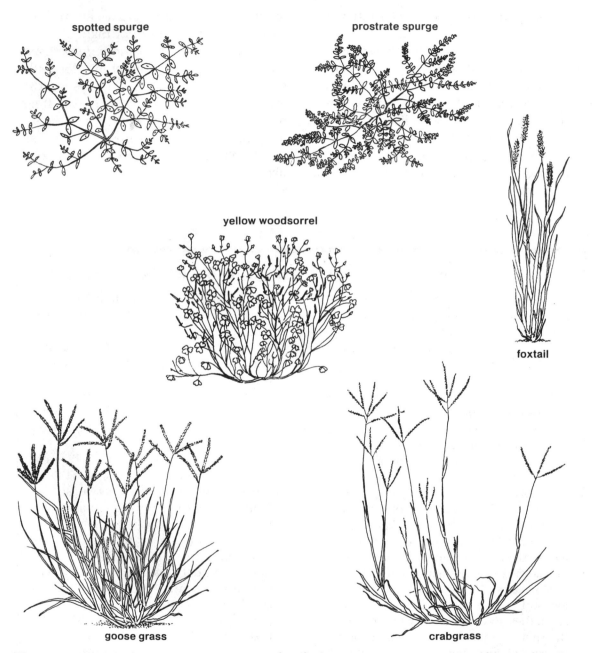

spotted spurge

prostrate spurge

yellow woodsorrel

foxtail

goose grass

crabgrass

Warm-season annual weeds, shown above and on facing page, appear in northern lawns when the grass is stressed by heat and drought and is at its weakest.

sandbur

common purslane

stink grass

switchgrass

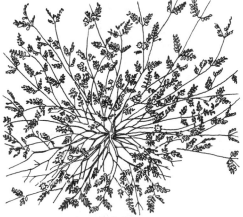

puncture vine

barnyard grass

close mowing, summer fertilization, and light, frequent watering. Control as for barnyard grass.

Yellow foxtail (*Setaria glauca*) and **green foxtail** (*S. viridis*) do not creep over the ground, but stand erect. The green foxtail's leaves have a hairy upper surface, while those of the yellow foxtail do not. Yellow seed heads mature in the fall. Foxtail likes adequate soil moisture, plenty of light, closely mowed turf, and summer fertilization. With its erect habit, you might think that close mowing would help to control foxtail. Not so. Foxtail likes low mowing. Remove clippings when seed heads are present. Aerate in spring. Fertilize in fall or spring.

Stink grass (*Eragrostis cilianesis*) is an erect but lower-growing foxtail. The seed head is finely branched. It is most easily identified by its pungent aroma. Seed germinates in the spring. The weed likes compacted soils, and can be controlled as for foxtail.

Witchgrass (*Panicum capillare*) is a wide-leaved, hairy bunch grass. Seeds germinate in the spring. It grows in freshly sown turf, but is discouraged by sowing new lawns at the proper time. Pull young witchgrass plants. Mow turf high in spring.

Sandbur (*Cenchrus pauciflorus*) has prostrate stems 6 inches to 2 feet long. Leaf blades are smooth and twisted, and the seed burrs are spiked. Seeds germinate in spring. Sandbur likes dry, sandy soils. Check its spread by improving the soil with organic matter, and fertilizing for vigorous turf.

Crabgrass (*Digitaria ischaemum*) has short, pointed, light green, hairy leaves borne on prostrate stems. Seed heads on the main stem have three to nine spikes. Seeds germinate from spring through fall, beginning when the soil temperature reaches 55°F and continuing with a new surge after rain or irrigation. Crabgrass is at its worst in thin turf, with frequent watering and low mowing. For controls, see the box, Three Ways to Beat Crabgrass, on page 131.

BROADLEAF WEEDS

Spurges, both prostrate (*Euphorbia supina*) and spotted (*E. maculata*), germinate at soil temperatures of 60° to 65°F, flower in May, and set seed July to October. They grow in rosettes, with stems radiating from a central taproot. Leaves are small and oblong, with a purple to red tint. Prostrate spurge occurs throughout the northern United States. Spotted spurge is more common in the eastern states. These weeds do best in drought-stressed, thin, undernourished turf. To control, pull them in spring and summer, while watering turf as deeply as necessary, and fertilize in fall.

Yellow woodsorrel (*Oxalis stricta*) looks somewhat like clover, with pale green heart-shaped leaflets in groups of three. Flowers are small and bright yellow. The plant is found throughout the United States, especially in thin turf and moist, fertile soils. Control by hand-weeding.

Common purslane (*Portulaca oleracea*) has fleshy, smooth stems that are red at the base. When broken, the stems secrete a clear juice. Leaves are oblong or egg-shaped and clustered. Purslane occurs throughout the United States, and likes hot, dry weather. Pull or hoe to remove the plants;

THREE WAYS TO BEAT CRABGRASS

Suppose you were told that you could reduce crabgrass to virtually nothing with no work, no chemicals, and no weeding. Hard to believe? It's true. Studies at the University of Rhode Island showed that high mowing alone reduced crabgrass cover on a test plot to virtually nothing in five years. And high mowing combined with heavy fertilization eliminated crabgrass in just one year.

The researchers were studying the combined effects of mowing, fertilization, and the herbicide bensulide on crabgrass. To their surprise, they learned that nonchemical control was just as effective, though perhaps not as speedy, in reducing the weed.

In the trial with unfertilized plots, the most significant factor was mowing height. A plot mowed at 1.2 inches reached a maximum cover of crabgrass, 54 percent, in the third year; the crabgrass dropped to 33 percent in the fifth year. But in a plot mowed at 2.2 inches, the crabgrass cover steadily decreased from a high of 30 percent in the first year to 7 percent in the fifth year.

A combined program of heavy fertilization and high mowing really hastened the demise of the crabgrass. One plot received nitrogen fertilizer in three applications, one-half in November, one-quarter in June, and one-quarter in September. When that plot was mowed at 2.2 inches, crabgrass coverage dropped to 8 percent the first year, and continued to decline to just 2 percent after five years.

Another study showed that fertilizing alone, at the proper time in the right amounts, will work almost as well. The study is a venerable one, performed 50 years ago by the Ohio Extension Service, before herbicides were in vogue. The researchers found that simply applying poultry manure at a rate of 20 pounds per 1,000 square feet, in late fall and again in early spring, reduced crabgrass by as much as 75 percent the following year. The fertilizer allowed the grass to get off to a vigorous start in the spring and crowd out the weed.

Researchers have found another technique to eliminate crabgrass after it is established: shade. They covered a patch of badly infested bluegrass lawn with black mulching paper (black plastic would probably work just as well). When the plastic was removed after ten days, all of the crabgrass was dead. The bluegrass had yellowed, but it recovered quickly.

you can also control them by aerating the soil, and irrigating when necessary.

Puncturevine (*Tribulus terrestris*) has low, branching stems that may spread up to 5 feet. Leaves are 2 inches long, hairy, and divided into five to seven pairs of leaflets. Pale yellow flowers appear from July to September, and set seed from late July to October. Seedpods have sharp spines. This weed is found mainly in the southern states,

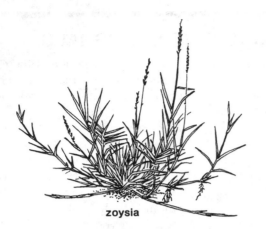

zoysia

nimble weed

yellow nutsedge

bermudagrass

Warm-season perennial weeds crop up in lawns that have been pampered with heavy summer fertilization and light watering.

WARM-SEASON PERENNIAL WEEDS

Weed Grasses

Bermudagrass
Dallisgrass
Nimble weed
Yellow nutsedge
Zoysiagrass

where it flourishes on compacted soils with low fertility. Chop or pull at taproots in spring or early summer. To discourage puncturevine, maintain good fertility, aerate the soil, and avoid compaction by replacing heavily traveled grass with paths.

WARM-SEASON PERENNIAL GRASSES

Warm-season perennials often occur in lawns that are stressed by summer heat and drought, and ironically, they also plague grasses that are pampered in the summer with heavy fertilization and frequent light watering. Dig out clumps and reseed. Mow high in summer. Fertilize in spring or fall. Water deeply only when necessary.

Nimble weed (*Muhlenbergia schreberi*) resembles creeping bentgrass in its habit. Leaves are light green or blue-green, and slow to color in the spring, resulting in straw-colored lawn patches early in the season. Nimble weed likes hot, dry conditions and thin, drought-stressed turf. Dig

out patches and reseed, and avoid summer fertilization.

Bermudagrass (*Cynodon dactylon*) is the most common of warm-season turfgrasses, and yet it is considered a weed in cool-season lawns. It is a fine- to medium-bladed grass. Although one of the fastest-growing grasses, bermudagrass is slow to green in the spring, and will be conspicuous as brown patches after the lawn has colored. It likes warm temperatures, compacted soils, and abundant moisture. To control it, pull the plants, remove roots, fertilize in fall, and don't water in summer.

Zoysia (*Zoysia* spp.) is yet another warm-season turfgrass that is a weed when it invades northern turf. The blades are fine and erect. It spreads slowly, greens late in the spring, and browns early in the fall. Zoysia grows best under warm, dry conditions, and can outdo other grasses in heavily trafficked areas. To rid your lawn of it, dig up clumps and reseed, and avoid summer watering and fertilization.

Dallisgrass (*Paspalum dilatatum*) is one of the most common weeds in southern lawns, especially in the Southeast. The coarse, yellow blades usually begin growing before lawns get started in the spring. It takes to fertile, well-irrigated soils. Dig up clumps and reseed. Avoid spring fertilization and watering.

Yellow nutsedge (*Cyperus esculentus*) is not a grass, but a sedge. Its coarse, light green to yellow leaves grow from triangular stems. It grows vigorously in summer, especially in moist conditions with close mowing, but it cannot stand a frost. To control it, mow high in early to midsummer. Water deeply and infrequently.

8

GETTING
THE BUGS OUT

Insects rarely trouble a healthy lawn. And the keys to a healthy lawn, as the other chapters of this book point out, include avoiding pesticides, using natural fertilizers, mowing properly, and selecting the right varieties. Given this help, natural predators will have a chance to build up their numbers and keep pests in check.

Many lawn pests are too small to notice when you're cruising along behind the lawnmower. Others spend most of their lives underground and out of sight. So you should make a practice of examining your lawn closely whenever you finish mowing. Check for insects and the telltale signs of their damage.

The first step in natural insect control on the lawn is learning not to overreact. You can't go running for the insecticide, even if it is organic, at the first sight of a bug. This means getting to know what the enemies look like and when to expect them. The point is to attack only when they're actually doing damage to your lawn.

A second measure is to add a variety of vegetation to encourage beneficial insects and birds to take up residence in and around the lawn. A lawn is by nature a monocrop. And monocrops, as agribusiness knows, invite pestilence. Although there's no such thing as companion planting when it comes to turf, you can cut down on pests by bordering and dotting your yard with trees and shrubs to attract these natural allies.

Trees, flowering shrubs, and berry bushes are popular habitats for grub-eating birds. Flower borders and beds will attract predators like the big-eyed bug, which preys on chinch bugs. Many beneficial insects feed on the nectar from umbelliferous plants like Queen Anne's lace and composites like daisies. Other favorites are the herbs caraway, coriander, dill, and fennel, as well as the flowers of black-eyed Susans, buttercups, strawflowers, sunflowers, and yarrow. Your lawn doesn't have to be taken over by these plants. The beneficials will patrol for bugs as far as 50 yards from their favorite nectar-

(continued on page 140)

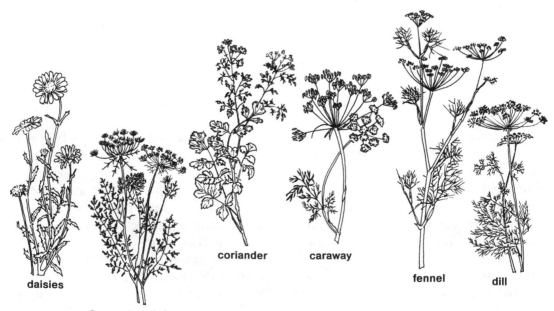

daisies

Queen Anne's lace

coriander

caraway

fennel

dill

Wildflowers, such as daisies and Queen Anne's lace, and umbelliferous herbs provide food for beneficial insects.

A GARDENER'S AVIAN FRIENDS

Region	Bird	Season Birds Are Present	Pests Eaten	Some Native Plants for Food and/or Shelter
Northeast	American goldfinch	All year	Some aphids and caterpillars	Balsam fir, spruce, pine, garden flowers
	Black-capped chickadee	All year	Eggs of moths and plant lice, caterpillars, flies, leafhoppers, treehoppers	Pine, hemlock, birch
	Downy woodpecker	All year	Wood-boring larvae of beetles, moths, adult beetles and ants	Various oak varieties, hop hornbeam, dogwood
	Evening grosbeak	Winter	Some beetles, caterpillars	Maple, dogwood, wild cherry
	Rufous-sided towhee	All year	Beetles, moths, caterpillars, grasshoppers	Dogwood, oak, huckleberry, wild blackberry
	Slate-colored junco	Summer in northern states, winter in southern states	Caterpillars, beetles, ants, other insects	Sumac, pine, native grasses, weeds
	White-breasted nuthatch	All year	Beetles, weevils, ants	Oak, pine
Midwest	American goldfinch	All year	Some aphids, caterpillars	Native garden flowers, weeds, grasses, conifers
	Brown thrasher	All year	Beetles	Dogwood, oak, hawthorn
	Eastern bluebird	All year	Ground beetles, weevils, caterpillars, sowbugs, other insects	Dogwood, hackberry

(continued)

A GARDENER'S AVIAN FRIENDS—Continued

Region	Bird	Season Birds Are Present	Pests Eaten	Some Native Plants for Food and/or Shelter
Midwest— *(continued)*	Mockingbird	All year	Beetles, ants, bees, wasps, grass-hoppers	Dogwood, cedar, hackberry, hawthorn
	Robin	All year	Caterpillars, beetles, sowbugs, termites	Dogwood, huckleberry, hawthorn
	Slate-colored junco	Winter	Caterpillars, beetles, ants, other insects	Native grasses, weeds
	Yellow-shafted flicker	All year	Ants, beetles, caterpillars, other insects	Oak, dogwood, native fruit-bearers
Northwest	American goldfinch	All year	Some aphids and caterpillars	Filaree, oak, native grasses, weeds
	Evening grosbeak	All year	Some beetles, caterpillars	Dogwood, cedar, hemlock
	Pine siskin	All year	Caterpillars, aphids, true bugs and fly larvae	Pine, weeds
	Red-shafted flicker	All year	Ants, beetles, grasshoppers, crickets	Oak, grape, elderberry
	Robin	All year— more common in summer	Caterpillars, beetles, sowbugs, termites	Raspberry, grape, dogwood
	Steller's jay	All year	Wasps, beetles, grasshoppers	Oak, elderberry, raspberry
	White-breasted nuthatch	All year	Beetles, weevils, ants, moths, caterpillars	Oak, pine

Region	Bird	Season Birds Are Present	Pests Eaten	Some Native Plants for Food and/or Shelter
Southeast	Cardinal	All year	Caterpillars, grasshoppers, true bugs, beetles	Native fruit-bearers, grasses
	Eastern bluebird	All year	Ground beetles, weevils, caterpillars, sowbugs, other insects	Native fruit bearers
	Red-bellied woodpecker	All year	Beetles, ants, caterpillars, true bugs	Pine, oak
	Robin	All year	Caterpillars, beetles, sowbugs, termites	Black gum, native fruit-bearers
	Slate-colored junco	Winter	Caterpillars, beetles, ants, other insects	Grasses, pine, weeds
	Tufted titmouse	All year	Caterpillars, wasps	Oak
	White-breasted nuthatch	All year	Beetles, weevils, ants, moths, caterpillars	Oak, pine
Southwest	Berwick's wren	All year	Great variety of insects including weevils	Native underbrush, thickets, pinyon, juniper
	Bullock's oriole	Summer	Caterpillars, beetles, ants, wasps	Shade trees such as oak, dogwood, elderberry
	Chipping sparrow	All year in southern states, summer in northern states	Grasshoppers, caterpillars, beetles, leafhoppers, true bugs, ants, wasps	Filaree, native grasses and weeds, evergreens

(continued)

A GARDENER'S AVIAN FRIENDS—Continued

Region	Bird	Season Birds Are Present	Pests Eaten	Some Native Plants for Food and/or Shelter
Southwest— (***continued***)	Downy woodpecker	All year	Adult beetles, wood-boring larvae of beetles and moths, snails, aphids, scales	Large shade trees, pine, other evergreens
	Lesser goldfinch	All year in southern states, summer in northern states	Some caterpillars, aphids	Native grasses and weeds, filaree, sunflower
	Mockingbird	All year	Beetles, ants, bees, wasps, grasshoppers	Native underbrush, hackberry, elderberry, honeysuckle
	Rufous-sided towhee	All year	Beetles, moths, caterpillars, grasshoppers, bees, wasps	Native underbrush and weeds, oak, native fruit-bearers

Reprinted from NATURE'S DESIGN by Carol A. Smyser © 1982 by Rodale Press, Inc.

producers. Borders along the edge and an occasional island bed should be enough to fuel the ecosystem.

If pests do appear, or if you've inherited a chemical lawn that you're trying to set straight, there are natural controls, both biological and physical, that wipe out every turf pest. Some are long-term diseases that control pests year after year. Others are one-shot, quick-kill remedies.

Recommendations are given in the rest of the chapter, but please use these as a last resort. Spray only if your lawn is being seriously damaged by an insect that you have definitely identified, and only after you have exhausted all other means. A nonspecific, albeit organic, pesticide like neem or pyrethrum will knock out beneficials too, upsetting the balance and possibly leading to greater pest problems. If you see a billbug, leave it alone; if you discover a bunch of billbugs actually harming your lawn, *then* take steps against them.

AN ALL-SEASON PEST

Chinch bugs are season-long lawn pests throughout the country. They overwinter as adults in both the North and the South, and may emerge as early as March. Once they're up, they feed primarily on Kentucky bluegrass, fine fescues, bentgrass, St. Augustinegrass, and zoysia. The adults are $1/6$ inch long and orange-brown to black. They inject a salivary fluid into grass plants as they feed on the stems and leaves. Infested grass turns yellow and eventually dies in patches.

However, it's not the adults that do the most damage. That distinction belongs to the nymphs. When they first hatch, they are about half the size of a pinhead, and are bright red with a white band across the back. After having shed their skin four times, they wind up being black with white markings. A second generation is born in early fall, and it may be the most troublesome.

Chinch bugs have an offensive odor, especially when crushed, and a severely

BUG TIMETABLE

The first step in identifying an insect is learning what is likely to appear when. The following chart tells when the most common lawn pests show up, in both cooler and warmer regions of the country.

Cool-Season	Warm-Season
Late Winter (Mar.)	
Chinch bug	Chinch bug
Billbug	Billbug
Grubs	Grubs
Black turfgrass ataenius	Mole cricket
Greenbug	—
Sod webworm	—
Spring (Apr.-May)	
Chinch bug	Chinch bug
Billbug	Billbug
Black turfgrass ataenius	Mole cricket
Sod webworm	Sod webworm
Cutworm	Cutworm
Greenbug	Fire ants
Mites	—
Summer (June-Aug.)	
Chinch bug	Chinch bug
Billbug	Billbug
Grubs	Grubs
Black turfgrass ataenius	Mole cricket
Fall armyworm	Sod webworm
Greenbug	Fall armyworm

(continued)

BUG TIMETABLE—
Continued

Cool-Season	Warm-Season
Summer (June-Aug.) — *(continued)*	
—	Fire ants
—	Scale
Fall (Sept.-Oct.)	
Chinch bug	Chinch bug
Billbug	—
Grubs	—
Black turfgrass ataenius	—
Sod webworm	—
Greenbug	—

infested lawn has a smell that can be detected simply by walking across it. There are other ways to tell if you have a chinch bug problem, too. If you suspect an infestation, cut both ends off a coffee can, press it firmly into the grass, and fill it with water. If there are any chinch bugs present, they will float to the surface within five minutes. Fewer than 20 in the coffee can indicates that you have no problem. That density is not enough to damage the lawn. If the number is near 20, however, you should monitor every week or two to keep track of the population level.

A BUG-FIGHTING FUNGUS

If the population exceeds the acceptable level, you have a few options. Scientists have discovered that the fungus *Beauvaria bassianna* attacks the soft areas of the insects and eventually kills them. Neem is also effective against chinch bugs—drench the turf with it. This natural insecticide is a new organic control that is made from a tropical tree that is native to India.

Chinch bugs prefer hot, sunny lawns, and you can discourage them by shading the lawn with trees or shrubs. Since chinch bugs are normally not a problem in well-irrigated lawns, good watering will help reduce populations. It has also been shown that cutting back on nitrogen fertilizer will help limit chinch bug damage.

Finally, if you're planning to reseed your lawn and have had problems with chinch bugs, choose one of the resistant varieties of grass, such as the 'Floratam' variety of St. Augustinegrass.

THE WICKED WEEVIL

Billbugs get their name from a long snout that ends in a set of mandibles. But the adult weevils aren't the troublemakers. The larvae cause most of the damage to lawns, especially Kentucky bluegrass.

Adult billbugs are ¼ to ½ inch long and brown or gray. They overwinter as adults, emerging in April or May to lay eggs on the stems of lawn grass in May or June. The grubs that soon emerge are small, ⅝ inch long, legless, and white with yellow-brown

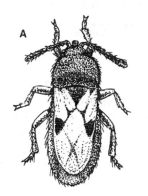

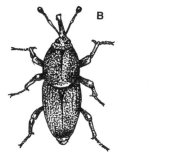

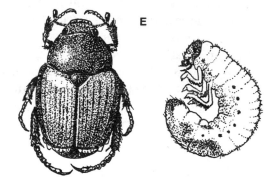

(A) Adult chinch bugs are orange-brown to black. (B) Billbugs are brown or gray, ¼- to ½-inch-long weevils. (C) Billbug larvae are tiny white-and-brown grubs that resemble puffed wheat. (D) Grubs: White grubs, the larvae of many beetles, measure from ¼ to ¾ inch in length. (E) Japanese beetles are ½ inch long, with metallic green or blue bodies and coppery wing covers. (F) Japanese beetle grubs are about 1 inch long, with white bodies and brown heads. Black turfgrass ataenius are ¼-inch-long, shiny beetles.

heads — they look something like puffed rice. They feed on stem tissue, causing infested shoots to turn brown and die. Then, as the heat sets in around June, the grubs move into the soil and feed on roots and rhizomes. They start out just below the thatch layer, then travel deeper as the soils dry. In late summer, the larvae pupate and adults emerge.

GRASS VS. BILLBUGS

If billbugs are present, you may spot the adults on sidewalks and driveways in May and June. Just one adult billbug or ten larvae per square foot of lawn indicates a problem population. Grass will appear brown and drought-stressed in June and July if billbugs are feeding heavily. Billbugs thrive in dry, stressed grass. To build a billbug-resistant lawn, correct compaction by aerating; water deeply in the spring to force grass roots downward; remove thatch; and add organic matter to the soil to hold moisture. On new lawns, plant resistant varieties.

Neem will kill both grubs and adults. An application of diatomaceous earth early in the season will control the adult bugs.

A GRUBBY THREAT

White grubs feast on the roots of Kentucky and annual bluegrasses, bentgrasses, and tall and fine fescues. They are the larval stage of scarab beetles, june bugs, rose and other chafers, and Asiatic and Oriental beetles, among others. Their C-shaped bodies measure from ¼ to ¾ inch long and are

RESISTANT GRASSES

Several varieties of perennial ryegrass are resistant to greenbug, armyworm, billbug, cutworm, and sod webworm. Those bugs just won't bother them. They are, roughly in order of most to least resistant: 'Repell', 'Citation II', 'Pennant', 'Regal', 'Commander', 'Sunrise', 'Prelude', 'Cowboy', 'All Star', and 'Premier'. The tall fescue variety 'Apache' has also shown some resistance to these pests.

blunt-ended and creamy white, with hard yellow or brown heads.

Overwintering grubs feed mainly on grass roots early and late in the season — April and May, and again in September and October. There may be one or two generations per year. When white grubs are feeding, the turf develops a spongy feel. Patches of turf can be pulled up easily from the soil, and brown patches develop. You'll see the adult beetles feeding on ornamentals and laying eggs in June and July.

If the lawn shows brown patches and loose sod in late spring or late summer, rake off all the loose turf and turn over the soil below. A population density of more than five grubs per square foot means it's time to take action. Continue to turn up the sod every few days until late fall. Birds will make short work of the exposed grubs. For long-term control, make your lawn an attractive habitat for birds by planting trees and shrubs that provide shelter and food.

GRUB CONTROL

You can control next year's grubs this year by reducing the beetle population in your yard. Handpick them early in the day and drop them into a bucket of water with a little kerosene floating on top. If beetles blanket your yard, apply pyrethrum early in the morning while they are sluggish.

An application of diatomaceous earth over the lawn will control surface-feeding grubs. Neem, an extract of the neem tree sold as Margosan-O, is a potent grubicide. The latest breakthrough in grub control is the use of predatory nematodes. These microscopic parasites attack and kill grubs, cutworms, and other pests. They are sold in a solution known as Scanmask, which you spray over the lawn when grubs are present. The parasites will search out and kill the grubs within a matter of days. One pint of Scanmask treats about 200 square feet of lawn.

When a lawn is infested with grubs, you can limit the damage they cause by watering lightly and frequently. This offsets the difficulty the grass has in picking up moisture through its damaged roots.

THE BATTLIN' BEETLE

Japanese beetles are a special case. The mature grubs are 1 inch long and white with brown heads. The pests overwinter deep in the soil as grubs, which begin feeding below ground in early spring. They pupate in midsummer, and adults emerge from the soil to feed and search out moist areas to lay eggs. Keeping your lawn dry will discourage them. The adults are active for about six weeks.

Do all that you can to limit the numbers of adults. Handpick the beetles in the morning as they congregate on plants, and drop them into a bucket of water with a film of kerosene on top. If the infestation is serious, dust them with neem, or apply Safer's Japanese Beetle Spray, which contains pyrethrum. By limiting the number of adults, you limit the number of subsequent grubs that can damage your lawn.

Don't use Japanese beetle traps. A study at the University of Kentucky showed that the traps attract more insects than they trap. On a typical morning, the researchers found that a trap attracted 119 beetles, but trapped only 65 of them. The rest were free to feed and lay eggs. The study concluded that the traps are more harmful than beneficial in the home landscape.

In spring and fall, check for grub damage by peeling back patches of sod. If you find more than a dozen per square foot, it's time to act. As with other grubs, nematodes and neem are effective controls. But there's also a biocontrol especially for Japanese beetle grubs.

SPORES TO THE FORE

Milky spore, the venerable *Bacillus popilliae* disease, was one of the first popular biological controls, and it's still doing the job. In the half-century that the disease has been used, the beetles have yet to develop any resistance to it. The grubs die after their clear blood turns a milky white. The disease is harmless to humans and other warm-blooded animals, as well as to plants.

The spore dust is made by collecting grubs and inoculating them with the disease. Treatments are most effective when applied on a community-wide basis, in parts of the country where soil temperatures remain above 70°F for several months so that the disease can build up. Given these conditions, the disease takes about a year to establish itself; otherwise it may take three to five years to build up enough to infect an entire population of grubs.

You may apply the dust at any time the grubs are present, except when the ground is frozen or in a strong wind. Use 4 ounces per 1,000 square feet, applying the dust to spots 10 feet apart throughout the lawn. For faster results, you can double the dose and halve the distance between application spots. After applying, water the lawn lightly.

A TEENY-US?

Black turfgrass ataenius is a species of beetle. The larvae, which do the damage, are less than one-quarter the size of other grubs. They are C-shaped and white with brown heads.

Shiny, black, ¼-inch-long adults overwinter beneath the soil. In the spring you'll see them flying over the lawn. They're most active during the hottest part of the day in late spring, when they lay their eggs. The grubs begin feeding shortly after hatching. A second generation may occur later in the summer.

Apply neem or pyrethrum to control the adults, and pyrethrum or diatomaceous earth for the grubs.

REGIONAL PESTS

Lawn pest problems vary across the country. Here are the most troublesome pests by region.

Northeast: Chinch bug, leafhopper, grubs, sod webworm, Japanese beetle

Southeast: Japanese beetle, sod webworm, armyworm, grubs, billbug, chinch bug

Gulf States: Chinch bug, mole cricket, armyworm, mites, sod webworm

Great Lakes: Grubs, aphids, mites

Midwest: Sod webworm, grubs, chinch bug, billbug, Japanese beetle, cutworm

Plains States: Billbug, sod webworm

Northwest: Cutworm, sod webworm, white grubs

Southwest: White grubs, chinch bug

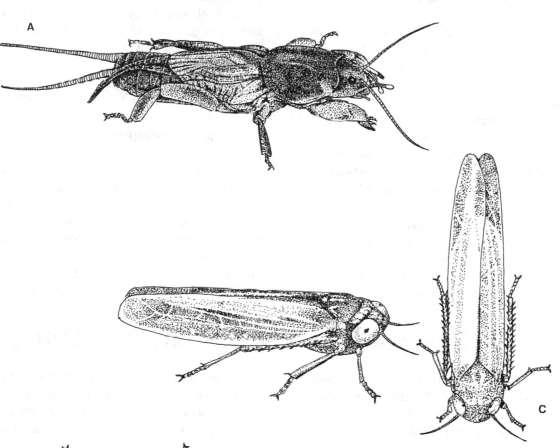

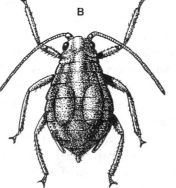

(A) Mole crickets are 1½ inches long, with short forelegs and shovel-like feet. *(B)* Green-bugs are a species of aphid. They are small, light green, and wedge-shaped. *(C)* Potato leafhoppers are ⅛ inch long, pale green, and wedge-shaped. They leave small white spots on lawns where they have been feeding.

A NEARSIGHTED PEST

Mole crickets are lawn problems mainly in the southern Atlantic and Gulf Coast states. They eat grass roots, but most of their damage occurs when their tunneling causes the soil to dry out. These tunnels are usually ½ inch in diameter and 6 to 8 inches below the soil surface.

The crickets are 1½ inches long and are light brown. They have short, stout forelegs, shovel-like feet, and large, beady eyes. The adults come to the surface in the spring to mate. Nymphs remain in the soil throughout the summer and fall.

Doom, the commercial form of *Bacillus popilliae*, is effective against mole crickets, as are predatory nematodes.

THE GRASS APHID

Greenbugs may be the most destructive species in the ubiquitous aphid family. They attack many agricultural crops; in lawns, they primarily infest Kentucky bluegrass.

Damage usually occurs first early in the summer. Areas where greenbugs are feeding turn a rusty color. These areas expand as the population increases. Sweep your hand over the grass—if they're present, you'll see them scatter.

These small, light green, wedge-shaped insects usually cause serious damage only in shaded areas. Even then, they rarely stay in one place long enough to do much harm to an actively growing lawn. If they do stay put, predators such as ladybugs and lacewings will eventually catch up with them. However, if you feel you can't wait, treat your lawn with insecticidal soap.

A HUNGRY HOPPER

Potato leafhoppers love alfalfa, but they'll snack on a lawn in a pinch. The ⅛-inch-long, pale green, wedge-shaped adults suck the sap from grass leaves, drying them out. A lawn under attack shows white areas. A closer look will reveal small white spots on the leaves where the pests have been feeding. Leafhoppers are worth controlling only on new lawns. A light dusting with pyrethrum will knock them out.

THE SIX-YEAR LUNCH

Wireworms are the hard-shelled larvae of click beetles. The brown, eellike worms grow to about 1½ inches over their lifespan of two to six years. They can damage turf by feeding on the roots, resulting in irregular areas of wilted grass.

Control of wireworms is generally not necessary if the soil is not overly wet. But if wilted patches reveal colonies of wireworms underneath, there are a few nonchemical steps you can take. Handpick and destroy adult click beetles when they emerge from the soil in the spring. The best way to beat the larvae is to trap them, taking advantage of the fact that they prefer most vegetables to grass roots.

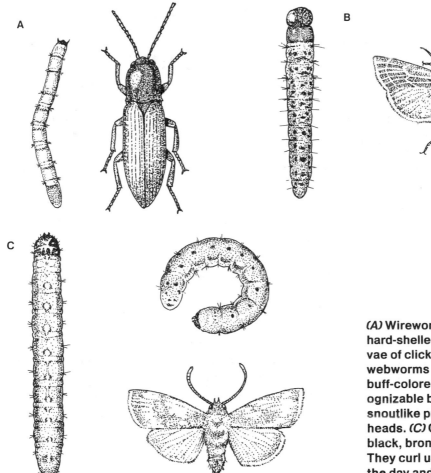

(A) Wireworms are brown, hard-shelled, 1½-inch-long larvae of click beetles. (B) Sod webworms are larvae of the buff-colored lawn moth, recognizable by the pair of snoutlike projections on their heads. (C) Cutworms may be black, bronze, or variegated. They curl up in grass during the day and feed at night.

Dig several holes in the lawn, each measuring about 3 inches wide and 3 inches deep. Remove the sod and place it aside. Bait each hole by jamming a stick through half of a potato and burying it in the bottom of the hole with the stick exposed as a marker. Check back in three or four days—the potatoes should be crawling with wireworms. Destroy the worms by tossing the potatoes in a bucket of water with kerosene floating on top. Then bait the traps again.

A SILK-SPINNER

Sod webworms prey on Kentucky bluegrass, bentgrass, tall and fine fescues, and zoysia. The worms are larvae of the buff-colored lawn moth, which you'll see at dusk in late spring flying zigzag fashion over the lawn. The moths are easy to identify by the pair of snoutlike projections on their heads and by the way they fold their wings close to the body when at rest.

The larvae overwinter in silk-lined burrows in thatch layers, and emerge as temperatures rise in spring. They have dark brown heads and dark spots scattered over the body. They feed at night on the leaves and stems of grass near ground level, leaving irregular brown spots of thinned turf.

The overwintering larvae mature to moths in mid-May to mid-June and produce another generation of larvae from late June to July. There may be as many as three generations each season.

More than 15 larvae per square yard means that it's time for control measures. The best long-term cure is to plant grass that is resistant to sod webworms. Short of that, dethatch the lawn to deprive larvae of their favorite dwelling place. Make sure that the soil is well-drained and that the grass has sufficient moisture to continue growing strongly. If you can't afford to wait for these measures to take hold, soak the lawn with a solution of 3 tablespoons of dishwashing liquid or insecticidal soap to 1 gallon of water. When the grubs float to the surface, remove and destroy them. Finally, *Bacillus thuringiensis* (Bt) is very

effective against the larvae (but not against the adult moths).

THE UNKINDEST CUT

Cutworms are familiar foes to anyone who has grown a vegetable garden. Though they prefer tender tomato, pepper, and broccoli plants, at least three species — the black, bronzed, and variegated cutworms — also munch on young grass leaves.

Cutworms are the larval stage of dark, night-flying moths. After they hatch, they curl up in the grass during the day and feed at night. Unless there is a severe infestation, they don't do a lot of damage. In fact, more damage is done to the turf by birds that scratch and claw to reach them.

It's not likely that you'll have a serious enough problem with cutworms to warrant treatment. But if necessary, an early evening application of pyrethrum will kill the bugs. Cutworms overwinter in trash and clumps of grass. To discourage them, clean up around the lawn. Mow the lawn closely in the fall and remove the clippings.

Bacillus thuringiensis (Bt) will infect the variegated cutworm. For others, a simple bait works wonders. Mix equal parts of hardwood sawdust and wheat bran with enough molasses to make a gooey substance, and add just enough water to make it sticky. Scatter the mixture around the lawn at dusk. The cutworms will find the molasses irresistible. The stuff clings to them as they crawl through it, then hardens so that they are helpless by morning. Since the worms are unable to burrow back into the ground, they make easy prey for birds and other predators. Predatory nematodes will also control cutworms.

MIGHTY MITES

Mites can cause a lot of damage for so small a pest. Chances are you won't realize you have them until they have become an infestation.

Bermudagrass mites suck the juice out of grass, turning it yellow or straw-colored. A heavy population will kill the plants, resulting in thinned, brown turf. You'll see the damage but not the cause, because you need a microscope to identify these tiny, white, eight-legged creatures.

Clover mites are a little bit bigger. Look closely, and they'll appear as dust crawling on the leaves. They feed mainly on clover, but will also invade turf. They are rust-colored, with long front legs.

The winter grain mite is a newcomer to lawns in the North. It has been known to damage Kentucky bluegrass, red fescue, fine fescue, and bentgrass. The eggs hatch in the fall. Adults are olive green with red legs; they can be seen with the naked eye. They do most of their dirty work in winter and early spring.

You can spot grain mite adults in the thatch during the winter. By early spring, their numbers may increase to over 1,000 per square foot, diminishing in late spring. Their damage resembles winterkill.

Control all mites with repeated applications of insecticidal soap. Mites are a problem mainly during hot, dry weather. Frequent light sprinkling of the lawn will keep their numbers down.

ANTSY GRASS

Fire ants can do a lot of backyard damage in the Gulf Coast states. Their tunnels and mounds can destroy a lawn. They are most frequently a problem in sunny sites and clay soils. Black ants, thief ants, and carpenter ants also build troublesome mounds in lawns.

Pouring liquid pyrethrum or insecticidal soap down the anthills will offer some control, but a homemade citrus potion may work better. The bitter chemicals known as limonoids, found in the peels and pulp of oranges, are poisonous to ants. Make a slurry of peels in a food processor, dilute it with orange juice, then pour it down the anthills.

A MUNCHING MILITIA

Armyworms are known for their voracious appetite for corn, but fall armyworms also rank among the worst lawn pests in the South. They can destroy a bermudagrass lawn, chewing the leaves down to the crowns to leave patches of ragged grass. They are the larvae of dark-winged, night-flying moths. In summer, a single moth lays batches of

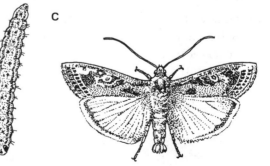

(A) Mites are tiny—some too small to see with the naked eye. They build fine webs on grass. *(B)* Fire ants are large red ants that build mounds on southern lawns. *(C)* Army-worms, resembling small cutworms, are larvae of dark-winged, night-flying moths.

180 or more eggs at a time on the grass. The moth then covers the egg groups with fuzz.

The newly hatched larvae are white with black heads. You may see them crawling, curled up on the leaves, or hanging from threads. They reach their full length of 1½ inches in less than a month. In the South, as many as six generations may occur in a year.

Neem is an effective control. Tachinid flies parasitize the caterpillars.

TIPPING THE SCALES

Scale insects are legless insects with a waxy shell. If you have a jade plant in your house, you've probably seen scale. And if you live in the South, you may have them on your lawn. Rhodes grass scale is found in California and the Gulf Coast States. It attacks grass crowns, making the plants wither and die. The ⅛-inch-long adults are purple-brown.

Bermudagrass scale feeds on bermudagrass stems, giving the crowns a moldy look. The white adults are ¹⁄₁₆ inch long. "Ground pearls" are scale insects that attack the roots of St. Augustinegrass, centipedegrass, and bermudagrass.

Repeated applications of insecticidal soap will control scale insects. Mix Safer's at 5 tablespoons to each gallon of water and wet the lawn thoroughly.

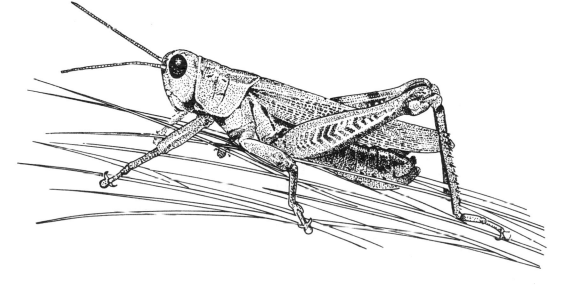

Grasshoppers often feed on lawns when field crops dry up.

A PLAGUE OF LOCUSTS

Grasshoppers can be turf pests in suburban areas near farms, especially in areas of the West where annual rainfall averages less than 30 inches per year. They will often migrate to backyards when field crops dry up, feeding on clovers and turfgrasses. In severe infestations, they can eat grass right down to the crowns. Don't panic if you see a few grasshoppers on your lawn. But if a swarm of them settles in and starts chowing down, it's time to do something. Handpicking works, especially early in the morning when they are still sluggish. Some gardeners have found that sprinkling the lawn in the morning slows the pests down even more and makes them easy to grab.

If grasshoppers are a problem on your lawn year after year, a good remedy is *Nosema locustae*, a disease that infects young grasshoppers. When grasshoppers eat the spores in bran bait, about half of them will die; others will pass on the disease to the next generation. Apply the bait in the spring at the rate of 1 or 2 pounds per acre.

9

DISEASE DIAGNOSIS AND CURE

You awake one morning to find that a patch of your lawn has turned brown. The patch seems to grow before your eyes. There are more patches the next day. Your lawn is clearly self-destructing. What do you do? Run for some fungicide? Make an emergency call to a lawn service company? Panic? To most of us, turf diseases are frightening because they are so mysterious. They often appear overnight, seemingly out of nowhere.

Many factors can trigger a disease outbreak on the home lawn: poor cultural practices, too much water, not enough water, too much fertilizer, not enough fertilizer, inadequate lime, soil compaction, excessive traffic, poor mowing practices, and perhaps most of all, too many pesticides and chemicals.

Luckily, there are many cultural ways to correct diseases, without resorting to still more chemicals. Mowing, watering, aerating, liming, proper fertilization—all can do a lot to cure an ailing lawn. And lawn diseases are relatively easy to handle.

Diseases become disasters only when turf is overmanaged. When chemicals are poured on the turf to boost grass growth or combat diseases and weeds, they take a toll. The lush growth caused by high nitrogen regimes makes grasses easy prey to disease. Fertilizers, herbicides, and fungicides all make their way into the soil, where they often destroy beneficial bacteria, upset the balance of the soil system, and give disease fungi a chance to get the upper hand. The result: more diseases, treated with more chemicals, and a less healthy soil. Eliot Roberts, director of the Lawn Institute, a seedmen's association, explains: "The more chemicals you use, the more you disturb the natural biological processes that convert organic matter into nutrients to keep the lawn going."

In fact, the more you mess with your lawn, the more apt you are to have disease problems; the more you neglect your lawn, the healthier it will be. It's only when you try to make your lawn perfect that diseases will be a problem. High-maintenance programs for turf are like an addiction. The more chemicals you use, the more you need.

Diseases are a sign that there's something seriously wrong with your lawn system. A home lawn can never be a completely natural self-sustaining ecosystem, any more than a field of tomatoes can be; but if a lawn is established properly and managed gently, there's no reason for disease to be a problem.

It's easy to understand why diseases occur when you look at the triangle of plant pathology. First, there's the disease agent itself; and for a lawn, a fungus is usually the culprit. Second, there's the host plant that's susceptible to the disease—the grass. Finally, conditions must favor the development of the disease, and this usually involves environmental or man-made stresses. If any one of those legs is missing, the disease can't strike.

In this chapter you'll learn how to break that triangle and keep it from reforming. If diseases do strike in the meantime, you'll also learn how to identify and eradicate them without chemicals.

NOT-SO-SECRET AGENTS

With the exception of one localized virus-caused disease—St. Augustine decline virus—all major turf diseases are caused by fungi. "Disease-causing organisms are always present in the lawn, ready to infect weakened plants when conditions become favorable," Eliot Roberts says. The chemical approach is to blast the fungi out of existence. But that's a hopeless battle. "Trying to kill the fungi does little good," he says, "because complete control is never possible." Nor is it desirable. About 100 different disease-causing fungi have been reported on turfgrass. Take a soil sample from any lawn, anywhere, and chances are good you will find five pathogenic fungi.

The soil itself can keep disease in check. In healthy soil, disease pathogens are vastly outnumbered by nonpathogenic microfauna (amoebas, nematodes, and insects) and microflora (bacteria, actinomycetes, and fungi). These nonpathogenic agents compete with the troublesome fungi for food and a niche in the ecosystem. They usually have the upper hand, and keep the disease-causing organisms in check unless outside intervention upsets the equilibrium.

A stress — perhaps the application of a toxic herbicide — may allow the disease organisms to surge, and they go to work on the lawn. You are apt to notice spots, patches, and discoloration. In time, if the stress is reduced and the soil is kept healthy, the soil will re-establish its equilibrium and the disease will probably disappear.

But the common solution is to go for the quick fix and use a fungicide. That may work for the short term, but in the long run it only makes the problem worse. Fungicides destroy the delicate balance of the soil. They not only suppress activity of those fungi that cause a target disease, but also are apt to have a greater effect on beneficial fungi and sometimes other helpful microorganisms as well. The result may be further outbreaks of disease.

Fungicides can also cause other disease pathogens to get the upper hand. Use a fungicide to kill off one of the five pathogenic fungi in a typical lawn, and chances are good that one of the other four will exert itself once the balance has been broken.

In effect, fungicides often force you to trade one disease for another.

Technical papers show more than 90 examples of turfgrass diseases that have been made more severe as a result of fungicide applications. For example, brown patch, stripe smut, and red thread have all been *enhanced* by applications of such common fungicides as benomyl, chloroneb, cyclo-heximide, propiconazole, and thiram. Rusts, leaf spot, red thread, typhia, and pythium have all been *amplified* by benomyl. Dollar spot has *spread* after applications of maneb, thiram, and other fungicides. Dinoseb, a commonly used fungicide, has been shown to suppress beneficial soil microorganisms for as long as three months.

Because of this vicious cycle, grounds-keepers are constantly applying chemicals on golf courses, and why contract lawn services are a booming business. You can break the cycle by adding beneficial micro-organisms to your yard.

These microorganisms are already teaming in healthy, virgin, chemical-free soil; beneficial bacteria and fungi work to keep disease-causing fungi in check by competing with them for food. But plant pathologists at Michigan State University found that an additional booster of actinomycetes could rescue diseased turf. These microscopic plants are known primarily as decomposers of organic matter. They're responsible for the characteristic sweet smell of freshly worked soil.

The Michigan State researchers found that commercial organic fertilizers containing actinomycetes could help lawns recover from necrotic ring spot, dollar spot, and fusarium blight. The products also reduced thatch, a major contributor to the disease cycle.

There are other ways to increase the microorganism level of your soil. Applications of manure can greatly raise the actinomycete level in the soil. Top-dressing with compost, peat humus, and topsoil will do the same. Alternately, if you stop using chemical herbicides, insecticides, and fertilizers, as well as fungicides, the microorganism population will gradually build up on its own.

Seaweed is another good natural disease-fighter. The hormones found in it will act as fungal inhibitors. Studies at Clemson University in South Carolina showed that applications of liquid seaweed reduced fusarium and dollar spot in turf.

HOSTS WITH THE MOST

Grasses aren't the gracious hosts to diseases they once were. There has been a revolution in turf breeding in the past 30 years, all benefiting the homeowner. The field of horticulture has never seen anything like the recent proliferation of disease-resistant turfgrasses. It started with 'Merion' Kentucky bluegrass. This variety was discovered as a clump of grass growing in a golf course in the 1930s, and introduced commercially in the early 1950s.

'Merion' Kentucky bluegrass, with its resistance to drechslera leaf spot and crown rot, was called a miracle grass. But after it

was planted across the country, pathologists discovered that ophiobolus disease feasted on the new variety, and stripe smut could virtually wipe it out. It's still a decent lawn grass in some areas under certain conditions. But it pales in comparison to varieties that have come along since then. At last count there were 86 varieties of Kentucky bluegrass on the market, many of them virtually immune to diseases. Modern cultivars 'Adelphi', 'Eclipse', 'Touchdown', and 'Glade' are, like 'Merion', resistant to leaf spot, with improved resistance to stripe smut. The recent Kentucky bluegrass cultivars 'Park' and 'Kenblue' are especially reliable under low-maintenance conditions. They grow vigorously with minimal care and fertilizers.

Another striking breakthrough was the 1960s introduction of the first turf-type perennial ryegrass, 'Manhattan', so named because it was discovered in the middle of New York City's Central Park. Until then, perennial ryegrasses had been developed for forage rather than turf. But 'Manhattan', and later 'Pennfine', were finer-textured, more durable, and tolerant of disease. There are now more than 70 varieties of turf-type perennial ryegrass available, and virtually all of them are resistant to one or more diseases. For example, new varieties that show good resistance to net blotch and brown patch include 'Prelude', 'Palmer', 'Premier', and 'Manhattan II'.

All told, there are now more than 200 varieties of turfgrass that are resistant to at least one disease. Most of them carry multiple disease resistance. Chances are that if you have problems with a disease, there

DISEASE-RESISTANT GRASS VARIETIES

Leaf Spot and Melting Out

Fine Fescue: 'Reliant'

Kentucky Bluegrass: 'Bonnieblue', 'Challenger', 'Eclipse', 'Georgetown', 'Majestic', 'Midnight', 'Nassau'

Perennial Ryegrass: 'Belle', 'Blazer', 'Cowboy', 'Ranger'

Tall Fescue: 'Adventure', 'Brookston', 'Houndog', 'Jaguar', 'Mustang', 'Olympic'

Stripe Smut

Kentucky Bluegrass: 'Adelphi', 'Admiral', 'America', 'Apart', 'Aquila', 'Arista', 'Aspen', 'Banff', 'Barblue', 'Birka', 'Bonnieblue', 'Bristol', 'Brunswick', 'Campina', 'Campus', 'Challenger', 'Charlotte', 'Cheri', 'Columbia', 'Delft', 'Delta', 'Eclipse', 'Enmundi', 'Enoble', 'Escort', 'Geary', 'Georgetown', 'Geronimo', 'Glade', 'Holiday', 'Kenblue', 'Lovegreen', 'Majestic', 'Mona', 'Monopoly', 'Nassau', 'Nugget', 'Parade', 'Park', 'Pennstar', 'Plush', 'Ram I', 'Rugby', 'Shasta', 'Sodco', 'Sydsport', 'Touchdown', 'Trenton', 'Vantage', 'Welcome'

Powdery Mildew

Fine Fescue: 'Dawson', 'Fortress', 'Gracia', 'Reliant', 'Reptans', 'Ruby'

Kentucky Bluegrass: 'Aquila', 'Cello', 'Cougar', 'Kenblue', 'Mystic', 'Palouse', 'Primo', 'Ram I', 'Sodco', 'Welcome'

Leaf Rust

Kentucky Bluegrass: 'Aquila', 'Arista', 'Bonnieblue', 'Columbia', 'Cougar', 'Delta', 'Enoble', 'Fylking', 'Geary', 'Georgetown', 'Glade', 'Kenblue', 'Majestic', 'Palouse', 'Parade', 'Park', 'Pennstar', 'Prato', 'Primo', 'Rugby', 'Sodco', 'South Dakota Common', 'Trenton', 'Windsor'

Perennial Ryegrass: 'Delray', 'Elka', 'Ensporta', 'Fiesta', 'Prelude', 'Wendy'

Dollar Spot

Fine Fescue: 'Agram', 'Barfalla', 'Biljart', 'Checker', 'Encota', 'Famosa', 'Koket', 'Reliant', 'Scaldis', 'Shadow', 'Tournament'

Kentucky Bluegrass: 'Adelphi', 'America', 'Aquila', 'Arista', 'Bonnieblue', 'Bristol', 'Eclipse', 'Galaxy', 'Geary', 'Majestic', 'Midnight', 'Newport', 'Palouse', 'Parade', 'Park', 'Pennstar', 'Prato', 'Primo', 'Sodco', 'Windsor'

Perennial Ryegrass: 'Barry', 'Capper', 'Caravolle', 'Citation', 'Dasher', 'Ensporta', 'Exponent', 'Linn', 'Manhattan II', 'NK-100', 'NK-200', 'Regal', 'Rex', 'Sprinter', 'Venlona'

Red Thread

Fine Fescue: 'Argenta', 'Atlanta', 'Barfalla', 'Biljart', 'Boreal', 'Cascade', 'Centurion', 'Engina', 'Ensylva', 'Fortress', 'Gracia', 'Grello', 'Highlight', 'Jade', 'Pennlawn', 'Puma', 'Ranier', 'Ruby', 'Scaldis', 'Scarlet', 'Veni', 'Waldina', 'Waldorf', 'Wintergreen'

Kentucky Bluegrass: 'Adelphi', 'Admiral', 'Arista', 'Birka', 'Bonnieblue', 'Bristol', 'Campus', 'Cello', 'Challenger', 'Cougar', 'Delta', 'Dormie', 'Eclipse', 'Geary', 'Georgetown', 'Majestic', 'Monopoly', 'Nassau', 'Newport', 'Palouse', 'Primo', 'Sodco', 'Touchdown', 'Trenton'

Perennial Ryegrass: 'Acclaim', 'Barenza', 'Belle', 'Birdie', 'Blazer', 'Citation', 'Clipper', 'Dasher', 'Delray', 'Derby', 'Diplomat', 'Ensporta', 'Eton', 'Exponent', 'Fiesta', 'Goalie', 'Lamora', 'Linn', 'Loretta', 'NK-100', 'NK-200', 'Norlea', 'Perma', 'Player', 'Ranger', 'Regal', 'Score', 'Sprinter', 'Venlona', 'Wendy', 'Yorktown'

(continued)

DISEASE-RESISTANT GRASS VARIETIES— Continued

Fusarium Patch

Fine Fescue: 'Barfalla', 'Biljart', 'Jade', 'Jamestown', 'Koket', 'Scaldis'

Kentucky Bluegrass: 'Adelphi', 'Admiral', 'Birka', 'Bonnieblue', 'Fylking', 'Glade', 'Lovegreen', 'Monopoly', 'Nassau', 'Shasta', 'Victa'

Perennial Ryegrass: 'Barenza', 'Diplomat', 'Eton', 'Game', 'Lamora', 'Manhattan', 'NK-200', 'Norlea', 'Omega', 'Pelo', 'Pennfine', 'Sprinter', 'Wendy'

Brown Patch

Perennial Ryegrass: 'All Star', 'Barry', 'Citation', 'Delray', 'Manhattan II', 'Palmer', 'Pennant', 'Prelude', 'Premier', 'Yorktown II'

Tall Fescue: 'Brookston', 'Jaguar', 'Mustang', 'Olympic'

Typhula Blight

Perennial Ryegrass: 'Regal'

---

will be a lawn grass resistant to it.

Resisting diseases can be as simple as planting the right grass in the right place. Stressed grass is more susceptible to infection. A sun-loving variety planted in the shade is more likely to become diseased than a shade-tolerant variety planted in the same place. There are grasses suited to heavy traffic, drought, high moisture, and so on. Specific recommendations are given in Chapter 2.

OUTSIDE INFLUENCES

The third side of the disease triangle is the conditions that favor the growth of pathogenic (disease-causing) fungi. Some diseases kick in with cool weather, while others like it hot. Some like dry conditions, others like it wet. You're limited in how much you can modify environmental conditions—you can't lower the humidity or stop the rain, for example. But you can make sure that your lawn is at its healthiest and most resistant when those disease-favoring conditions happen to come along.

Ironically, a neglected lawn isn't the easiest prey for diseases. The more maintenance that's spent on a lawn, the more likely it is to be affected. There are several reasons for this.

■ Excessive nitrogen fertilizer forces grass to grow too fast and lush, and makes it easy prey for certain diseases; overfeeding also discourages earthworms and other microorganisms, which in turn increases thatch and the diseases harbored there.

■ Acid mineral fertilizers, like ammonium sulfate, favor fungi in the soil while discouraging bacteria and actinomycetes, both of which are proven fungi-fighters.

■ Excessive watering and foliar feeding will weaken root systems. Herbicides and fungicides destroy the life of the soil, allowing pathogens to get the upper hand.

TIPS FOR A HEALTHY LAWN

The New Lawn

1. Check drainage. If water puddles in spots, regrade and install drainage tiles.

2. Trim or remove shrubs or trees for good air movement and to reduce shade.

3. Add organic matter. Even if the soil appears to be in good shape, mix in 2 inches of peat moss, compost, leaves, or rich topsoil.

4. Test soil for fertility and pH, then correct if necessary. The pH should be near neutral (6 to 7). Soil should be moderately fertile.

5. Be aware of problem diseases. Check with Extension agents, garden centers, and neighbors to learn if any diseases are prevalent in the area.

6. Choose the right grass seed. Select varieties resistant to locally common diseases. Always use a mix of grasses to discourage the spread of disease. Choose shade-tolerant grasses for shady areas.

7. Give the grass a good start. Sow at the proper time (spring or fall), depending on your area. Sow at the proper thickness. Water when necessary.

8. Use groundcovers for problem areas like shade and slopes. Pave or make paths in heavy-traffic areas.

9. Establish and stick to a fertilizer schedule.

10. Remove weeds.

11. Regularly scout the lawn for problems.

The Established Lawn

1. If necessary, improve drainage.

2. Trim or remove trees or shrubs to reduce shade and increase air flow.

3. Top-dress.

4. Check thatch. If it is more than ½ inch thick, remove with a dethatcher or top-dress.

5. Check compaction. If soil is hard and compacted, repair by aerating.

6. Test soil for fertility and pH, then correct if necessary.

7. Establish and stick to a fertilizer schedule.

8. Stop using chemicals.

9. Overseed with resistant grasses or a different species. In California tests, mixing 15 to 20 percent turf type perennial ryegrasses with Kentucky bluegrass controlled fusarium blight on the bluegrass turf. Note past or current disease problems and choose new grasses accordingly.

10. Mow regularly.

11. Water thoroughly only when necessary, never in the evening.

12. Scout the lawn regularly and diagnose problems.

The most common lawn herbicide is 2,4-D, and it increases rust, fusarium, and helminthosporium disease.

■ Finally, frequent low mowing stresses the grass.

Of all the factors in the above list, low mowing may be the biggest culprit. Mowing too close will stress the plant, especially in hot and dry weather. Golf greens are a good example. Groundskeepers have to battle constantly against the familiar circles of brown patch. Because the grass is so closely cut, individual grass tips are closer together than on less severely mowed grass, enabling disease to spread more readily. At one golf course recently, the groundskeeper spotted what he thought was an entirely new disease. It looked like brown patch, but occurred in semicircles at the edge of the green. Finally someone figured out that the disease was indeed brown patch, but the fungus was spreading only to the edge of the green, stopping at the fairway where the grass was higher.

Even if you mow at the proper height, you may be spreading disease. If a disease isn't able to spread, it won't be a problem: Single plants may become infected, but when they die, the disease expires with them. But diseases colonize other plants when spread by walking or mowing, especially when the grass is wet. That's a good reason to keep the mower in the garage until the grass is dry. Generally, stay off diseased lawns whenever possible.

However, under certain conditions, mowing can help. Some diseases, brown patch and fusarium among them, attack the tips of blades and don't travel down toward the crown much. Mowing removes the affected site, so the disease is cut off and withers with the clippings.

HOW TO BE A DISEASE DETECTIVE

There are many cultural means to control, lessen, and even eliminate diseases. Fertilizaton, mowing, and watering all play a part. But before you can begin to deal with a disease, you have to know exactly which one it is.

Recognizing turf diseases is a tricky business. Plant pathologists spend careers studying the differences among diseases, some of which can be positively identified only under microscopes in the lab. But anyone can learn to pick out the most common diseases by recognizing symptoms and keeping track of the conditions under which they occur.

Turf disease diagnosis is an art, according to Patricia Sanders, associate professor at Pennsylvania State University. "You have to learn how to notice things," she says. "It takes an ability to think with an open mind. You have to look at a great many things."

Sanders says the good diagnostician collects as much information as possible before making a decision. Consider the environment, temperature, soil moisture, fertility, pests, drainage, topography, sun, and shade. Look at the general condition of the turf, the affected patches, and finally the blades of grass.

Symptoms are the evidence that the plant offers concerning the disease. There are basically two types: symptoms on the turf, and symptoms on the individual grass plant.

The turf symptoms can take many shapes and forms: spots, as in dollar spot; patches, as in red thread; rings, displayed by fusarium and fairy ring; circles, as in brown patch and snow mold; and an irregular pattern, in pythium blight. Or the diseased area may lack a pattern, as is true of powdery mildew and melting out.

That sounds simple and definitive. But often these turf symptoms are not well defined. The spots may run together and form a patch, or rings may resemble circles. Or a disease may start out as a ring and become a circle.

That's why it's also important to take a close look at the grass blades in the affected patch. Symptoms there can take many forms as well. There can be spots, stripes, random decay, stunting, wilting, or discoloration.

Some symptoms are easy to recognize on the grass. Fungi are visible on the blades when certain diseases strike. Powdery mildew shows white spores piled on the blades. Red thread disease looks like it sounds; infected plants bear thin threads of reddish mycelium. The sign of pink patch is

Powdery mildew is easy to diagnose. It shows up as white spores on the grass blades.

When infected with red thread, grass plants display thin threads of red mycelium.

just as distinctive, although more difficult to see; infected grass has pink, cottony growths that look a bit like cotton candy.

Stripe smut is a vicious-sounding disease. But again, the name helps by telling you what to look for. Black stripes between leaf blades are a sure sign that the grass has this disease. If you reach down and rub your hand over the infected grass, your fingers will come away sooty. Rust disease, on the other hand, releases a red soot that rubs off.

Keep in mind that your lawn problem may not be caused by disease, but by environmental stress or an injury. The problem could be drought; scalping from a lawnmower; herbicide or fertilizer burn; or even dog damage.

PUBLIC ENEMY #1

Brown patch (*Rhizoctonia solani Kuhn*) is the most widespread lawn disease in the United States, occurring everywhere but the Pacific Northwest. It attacks all species of lawn grass. If you've had a disease on your lawn, chances are that it was brown patch. Kentucky bluegrass is rarely damaged severely by the disease, but it is not immune. In the North, bentgrass is hit hard, as is St. Augustinegrass in the South.

Brown patch normally occurs during the summer on cool-season grasses, and in spring and fall on warm-season grasses. Hot, humid weather brings it on, and 80° to 85°F is the optimal range for its development. Highly fertilized grasses are especially susceptible. Brown patch occurs frequently and is especially virulent on highly maintained turf.

This disease lives up to its name. Circular patches measure from a few inches to several feet in diameter. At first, the grass in the patch appears dark and water-soaked. Eventually the grass dies and turns a characteristic brown. On coarse grasses such as ryegrass, the disease may appear as light-colored circles with brown edges, a configuration called frog's-eye patches.

DOWN THE DRAIN

If brown patch occurs regularly on your lawn, suspect poor drainage. Should that be the case, fungicides won't cure the problem. They may make matters worse by inhibiting the life of the soil, both chasing out earthworms and slowing the decom-

Black stripes on the leaf blades are a sure sign that stripe smut has taken hold.

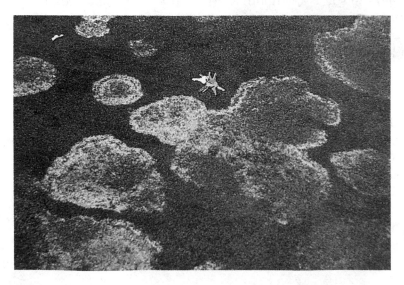

The brown circles of brown patch disease show up in hot, humid weather.

position of organic matter that aerates the soil. The drainage has to be improved. Short of tearing up the lawn and installing drainage tile, you can accomplish this by incorporating organic matter to loosen the soil. Top-dressing (see Chapter 4) adds organic matter and reduces the incidence of brown spot. Withholding nitrogen will also help. If hot, humid weather sets in for long periods, you can battle the disease by dragging a rope or garden hose over the lawn in the morning to remove the dew.

FOR A
FEW DOLLARS MORE

Dollar spot (*Sclerotinia homeocarpa*) also occurs in summer, but the conditions favoring it are almost completely the opposite of those behind brown patch. Dollar spot is most apt to strike when the soil is dry and low in nitrogen. The warm days and cool nights of early and late summer are apt to encourage it, and the optimal temperature range is 60° to 80°F.

If you see the disease patches at the right time, they will look like round, bleached spots about the size of a silver dollar. Look for a circle with a bleached center and brown margins. But the problem with diseases is that they don't always hold still long enough for you to diagnose them. Dollar spot offers a good case in point. As the disease develops, the spots spread and begin to overlap. They lose their integrity and don't look like spots as much as blotches.

However, if you take a close look at the infected grass, there are some telltale signs, especially in the early morning. You should see white fluffy strands of mycelium on the turf. And at any time of the day, you'll see light tan, red-bordered lesions on the tips of the leaves.

Susceptible grasses include annual bluegrass, bahiagrass, bermudagrass, centipedegrass, colonial bentgrass, creeping bentgrass, Italian ryegrass, Kentucky bluegrass, red fescue, redtop, sheep fescue, St. Augustinegrass, velvet bentgrass, and zoysia.

THE NITROGEN CURE

Adequate nitrogen enables grass to recover from dollar spot, and the Michigan Cooperative Extension recommends frequent light applications of nitrogen during an infestation. Its program calls for ½ pound of pure nitrogen per 1,000 square feet per month during June, July, and August. A well-fed lawn is less susceptible. The University of Washington Cooperative Extension reports that activated sewage sludge reduces the disease more than any other form of nitrogen. Since dried-out turf is more susceptible, regular deep watering helps control the disease. However, watering late in the day or evening gives the disease a chance to get a foothold.

Regular high mowing can control the disease once it strikes. Cutting off the tips of the grass removes the infected area, slows the disease's spread, and enables the grass to recover quickly, especially if adequate nitrogen is present.

Regular drenching with sea plant extracts (such as liquid seaweed) has been shown to control dollar spot fungus in tests at Michigan State University.

NOT FOR SEWING

Red thread (*Laetisaria fuciforme*) and **pink patch** (*Limonomyces roseipellis*) are caused by related fungi. They are most serious in the Northeast and Pacific states, where they occur during the cool, wet weather of spring and fall. They can also occur as winter diseases of bermudagrass as far south as Mississippi. Temperatures in the 50s and 60s encourage red thread and pink patch. High humidity with dew, drizzle, and fog are essential components of the causal cycle.

As you might guess, the names offer some clues for diagnosis. Grass infected with red thread has rusty or red threads of mycelium extending from the leaf tips. Pink patch shows up as coral pink, gelatinous masses on leaves and sheaths. Both symptoms are most conspicuous when the grass is wet. On the turf, red thread and pink patch show up as circular patches of scorched leaf tips from 2 inches to 2 feet in diameter. Small patches are circular, but as they spread they may become irregular.

Grasses most susceptible to red thread and pink patch are annual bluegrass, bermudagrass, colonial bentgrass, creeping bentgrass, Kentucky bluegrass, perennial ryegrass, red fescue, and velvet bentgrass.

To control these fungi, make sure the turf has adequate nitrogen. Regular mowing removes infected leaf tips and lessens the severity of the disease. Lawns that have regular, deep watering tend to be less susceptible.

A YANKEE BLIGHT

Pythium blight (*Pythium aphanidermatum*) is primarily a disease of cool-season grasses in the North. It is most serious on bentgrass. However, it may occur in the South when lawns are overseeded with ryegrass in the winter.

Pythium is easier to diagnose now that researchers have identified several very specific climatic conditions that must be met before the disease can occur. In trials at golf courses in Pennsylvania and California, the appearance of pythium was always preceded by a warm day and a warm, moist night. The researchers developed a model for predicting the occurrence of pythium. It involves only two factors: a maximum temperature above 86°F, and a relative humidity higher than 90 percent for 14 hours, during which time the minimum temperature remains higher than 68°F.

If those weather parameters have been met, look for symptoms — circular spots from one to several inches in diameter. As they spread, they will grow together to form large, irregular clusters. The turf in the spots will look dark and water-soaked. Cottony mycelium may appear early in the morning, and the grass may also feel slimy.

Grasses most susceptible to pythium are annual bluegrass, bermudagrass, colonial bentgrass, creeping bentgrass, Italian ryegrass, Kentucky bluegrass, perennial ryegrass, tall fescue, red fescue, redtop, rough bluegrass, and velvet bentgrass.

Once pythium gets a foothold, it's almost impossible to stop. Pythium can destroy an entire stand of grass in just 24 hours. The best control is prevention. A calcium deficiency makes grass more susceptible to pythium, so add lime when necessary. Do not water in the evening. Prune surrounding trees and shrubs to increase air circulation and, if necessary, limit thatch.

TAKE-ALL

Ophiobolus patch (*Ophiobolus graminis*) is a disease you don't have to worry about saying or seeing unless you live in the Pacific Northwest. The fungus is most active there during the wet winter months, although the symptoms usually don't show up until the spring. The disease, sometimes called take-all patch, first shows up as bright brown patches of dead grass, and may be confused with fusarium at that time. But unlike fusarium, the stricken patches can be easily pulled from the ground. The diseased patches are a few inches in diameter at first, growing rapidly up to 2 feet. As they enlarge, the central portion is often invaded by weeds.

The disease most commonly affects annual bluegrass, colonial bentgrass, Kentucky bluegrass, perennial ryegrass, red fescue, redtop, rough bluegrass, tall fescue, and velvet bentgrass.

You can check the spread of ophiobolus by applying sewage sludge (such as Milorganite) as a fertilizer.

A POWDERY PROBLEM

Powdery mildew (*Erysiphe graminis*) is considered a minor disease, unless it

If straw-colored spots of reddish-brown grass appear on your lawn, suspect drechslera melting out.

strikes Kentucky bluegrass. The most susceptible variety of that species is 'Merion'.

Powdery mildew occurs during cool, humid, cloudy weather. It's frequently found in shady patches, especially if air circulation is poor. And it's intensified if high rates of nitrogen have been applied in those areas. Mildew appears first as small patches of white to light gray fungus on leaves and sheaths. Tissue under the patch becomes yellow. Turf turns dull white, as though dusted with flour, and a white powder can be wiped from the leaves. Besides Kentucky bluegrass, powdery mildew occurs on bermudagrass, red fescue, sheep fescue, and redtop.

Prune trees and shrubs in the lawn to reduce shading and improve air circulation. Use a moderate amount of fertilizer. Water only in the morning, and mow high and frequently. Sow resistant varieties.

MELTING OUT

Drechslera leaf spots (*Drechslera* spp., formerly *Helminthosporium* spp.) are a family of diseases that go by a number of common names: melting out, going out, leaf spots, zonate eye spots, brown blight, leaf blotch, and crown and root rots. There are a number of strains, often classified by the type of grass they infect. In fact, one or more of the species attacks every turfgrass in the country. Drechslera diseases are among the most destructive of all lawn diseases.

Melting out (*D. poae*, formerly *H. vagans*), also known as leaf spot, is perhaps the most common disease of this family. It usually attacks Kentucky bluegrass during periods of cool, moist weather in spring or fall. It is active during the entire year in New Jersey, but in Pennsylvania it is most prevalent in cool months of spring and fall.

Melting out first appears as straw-colored spots with reddish-brown to black borders. In the melting out stage, stems, crowns, and roots rot and become discolored. When the disease strikes, lesions appear as water-soaked areas. Spots may be ⅜ inches long and ⅛ inch wide. But the disease can be positively identified only by microscopic inspection of spores.

To control, avoid heavy applications of nitrogen fertilizer in hot weather. Water thoroughly (6 to 8 inches deep) and infrequently. Mow high (1½ to 2½ inches) and remove the clippings. Remove thatch. Plant a resistant variety, such as 'Merion', 'Cougar', or 'Newport' Kentucky bluegrass. Many fine fescues are susceptible.

A FEW MORE SPOTS

Other Drechslera diseases strike bentgrass and bermudagrass. *D. erthrospilum* is common on bentgrasses in the Midwest and central Atlantic states. *D. giganteum* occurs in southern states on bermudagrass. Both are recognizable by leaf spots. The first appear as tan-centered leaf spots, bordered by reddish-brown, and the disease imparts a smoky blue cast to the infected area. The latter occurs especially in spring and fall when grass is semi-dormant. The spots are small brown to purple lesions which become reddish-brown areas, then wither and die.

If leaf spot strikes during warm, wet weather, the threat can be reduced by

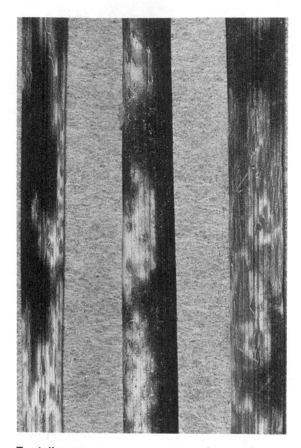

Rust disease appears as rusty red spores on the grass during cool weather.

CAST-IRON GRASS

Rusts (*Puccinia* spp.) can occur anywhere and strike any grass type. Rusts usually are found during late fall or early spring, but they are a major problem only in hot, dry weather when grass growth slows. The name is a good clue to diagnosis. Yellow to rusty red pustules of spores appear on infected grass. The rust material easily rubs off onto fingers, shoes, and clothing. If the disease becomes serious, grass turns yellow, then withers and dies.

Stressed grass is especially susceptible to rust, so follow a good fertility program. Watering should be thorough but infrequent, and never done in the evening. Plant resistant varieties. If rust strikes, mow frequently to remove diseased grass tips and spores.

STOP THAT SMUT

Stripe smut (*Ustilago striiformis*) usually occurs during the cool weather of spring and fall, when it turns the grass plants to pale green, yellow, or brown. You may see it on single plants, or in spots up to a foot in diameter. It's widespread throughout the United States, and is particularly destructive to Kentucky bluegrass.

At first, you may only notice that your lawn seems to be growing slowly. But if you look closely, you'll see black longitudinal stripes on the individual blades of grass. Eventually those stripes burst, releasing black powdery spores. The grass will then dry out and die.

slowing its spread by dew. Remove the dew by watering to wash the spores from the leaves, or wipe with a hose or rope. Follow the cultural practices recommended for melting out.

If smut strikes, mow frequently and remove the clippings. To reduce the chance of smut occurring, keep the lawn growing vigorously by maintaining a good fertilizer and water schedule. Plant resistant varieties. Among Kentucky bluegrasses, these include 'Belturf', 'Bonnieblue', 'Fylking', and 'Pennstar'. Tolerant varieties are 'Adelphi', 'Park', 'Sodco', 'Sydsport', and 'Warrens A-20' and 'A-34'.

A FUNGUS AMONG US

Fusarium blight (*Fusarium tricinctum*) is not the widespread disease it was once thought to be, even though fusarium is often the most abundant fungus species in grass during the summer. It was blamed for other diseases now known as summer patch and necrotic ring spot. Now, it's known that fusarium blight is largely restricted to the Midwest, California, areas of the Pacific Northwest, and the Mid-Atlantic states.

Fusarium blight occurs mainly on Kentucky bluegrasses, especially during periods of hot weather during July and August. The first sign is the appearance of discolored patches 2 to 6 inches wide that turn reddish-brown, then tan, then yellow. The spots often show up first along walkways and driveways where the turf is stressed. Look closely and you'll see that the roots and crowns have a dark rot and may show pink, fuzzy mycelium. In hot, humid weather, the disease can wipe out an entire lawn within a week.

The spores are most active when daytime temperatures are 85° to 90°F with night temperatures in the 70s. Although

Fusarium blight usually shows up first along walkways, driveways, or other dry areas of turf.

most damage occurs on bluegrasses (especially 'Merion' and 'Fylking'), bentgrasses and fescues are also quite susceptible.

The most common hosts of fusarium blight are annual bluegrass, colonial bentgrass, creeping bentgrass, Italian ryegrass, Kentucky bluegrass, perennial ryegrass, redtop, red fescue, rough bluegrass, sheep fescue, tall fescue, and velvet bentgrass.

Grass under stress is most susceptible. High nitrogen and low calcium levels also favor the disease. In areas where fusarium is a problem, avoid fertilizing in late spring or early summer. Mow high to reduce stress, and remove clippings that may be diseased. Remove thatch.

SNOW MOLD

Fusarium patch (*F. nivale*), also known as pink snow mold, is a worldwide problem, most serious in cool, moist climates such as that of the Pacific Northwest. If you catch it early, you'll be able to see very small (1- to 2-inch), circular, water-soaked spots on blades of grass. As they enlarge, they change from purple to tan and then white. They

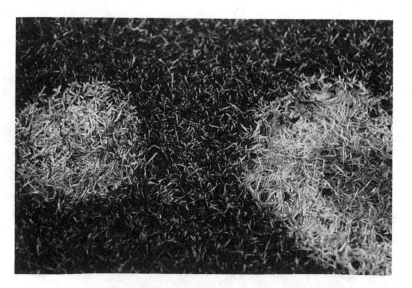

Fusarium patch develops under snow cover, and displays slimy patches of grass when the snow melts.

may also show a dense mass of mold which turns pink in sunlight. When the disease develops under snow cover, the patches will be larger, up to a foot or more. They will be matted together and feel slimy. The disease can occur in fall or spring. The optimum temperature for development is 32° to 40°F, but it has been known to occur at temperatures up to 88°. In the northern United States, the disease usually begins in the cool, wet fall and continues under melting snow. It can occur without snow, appearing as small circular spots similar to dollar spot.

To control, do not apply heavy nitrogen fertilizers or limestone in the fall. Remove thatch. Improve drainage and air circulation.

FROG-EYED LAWN

Summer patch (*Phialophora graminicola*) is another summer disease, spreading most rapidly when the temperature is 80° to 85°F and humidity is high. It often begins during hot, sunny days following prolonged rainy periods. Affected areas show patches of dead grass mixed with live plants. As the disease progresses, rings of dead grass form around healthy plants in a frog's-eye pattern.

Summer patch is encouraged by low mowing, heavy nitrogen fertilization, and excessively high or low pH. The best control is to eliminate all stresses. Feed the lawn with a well-balanced fertilizer, correct drainage of the soil, and water the lawn lightly during the hottest periods to reduce heat stress. Fine fescues, bentgrasses, and Kentucky bluegrasses are susceptible to this disease. 'Adelphi', 'Eclipse', 'Georgetown', and 'Monopoly' are resistant bluegrasses.

STRESSED-OUT SPOTS

Necrotic ring spot (*Leptosphaeria korrae*) could be known as the good-grass disease. It usually strikes dense, vigorous lawns, especially those that have been established from sod within the past five years. And when necrotic ring spot strikes, it really strikes. If dead spots appear out of the blue on a previously healthy lawn, suspect necrotic ring spot. In some cases the grass may not die, but will be stunted and turn yellow or red. The disease strikes from May to October, but is most severe from July to September.

The symptoms are virtually indistinguishable from summer patch. Even trained mycologists rarely can tell the difference. Fortunately, cultural control methods are the same. It's most important to eliminate any stresses. A light sprinkling of water in midday can be used to reduce heat stress. Infected grasses are most seriously affected when they are mowed short.

This fungus grows most rapidly from 60° to 80°F. However, its development makes identification difficult. It can kill grass roots without affecting the foliage, so the plants

Typhula blight appears as patches of white-coated grass after snowmelt.

could be severely infected without showing any symptoms—until environmental stress strikes, and the foliage suddenly dies, even though the infection might have occurred much earlier.

Ring spot is the predominant turf disease in Wisconsin, where it was first identified as something other than fusarium blight syndrome. It also ranks as one of the most important diseases of bluegrass in Washington State.

As yet, no varieties of bluegrass, bentgrass, bermudagrass, or fine fescue have been found tolerant to necrotic ring spot. However, perennial rye and tall fescue show good tolerance.

To control ring spot, mow high, and remove thatch by raking, verticutting, or top-dressing.

TYPHOID? NO, TYPHULA

Typhula blight (*Typhula incarnata*), also known as gray snow mold, occurs primarily in the northern United States and Canada when temperatures range from 32° to 40°F in late winter and early spring. It occurs most often on turf that has been covered by heavy, drifted snow that is slow to melt in the spring. When the snow does melt, it reveals damaged areas up to 2 feet in diameter and covered with white or light gray mycelium.

To prevent typhula, do not fertilize in the fall (except with sewage sludge). Mow short in the fall until snowfall and remove clippings. Do not compact the snow by skiing, snowmobiling, or other winter activities. Put up snow fences or windbreaks to prevent drifting of snow. Encourage early snowmelt by covering the snow with ashes, sewage sludge, or other dark material.

Gray snow mold most commonly strikes annual bluegrass, colonial bentgrass, creeping bentgrass, Italian ryegrass, Kentucky bluegrass, perennial ryegrass, red fescue, rough bluegrass, tall fescue, and velvet bentgrass.

MALEVOLENT MUSHROOMS

Fairy rings (*Marasmius oreades*) may sound innocent and even charming, but they can make a mess of a lawn. They are also among the most difficult of diseases to eradicate. However, they are not a common problem except in areas of high rainfall like the Pacific Northwest. Fairy rings typically first appear in the spring as circles of dark green grass. Eventually the grass may die either inside or outside the ring. After a rain, mushrooms may appear on the circumference of the circle.

Fairy rings are caused by mushroom mycelium growing in a circular pattern. As the mycelium breaks down organic matter in the soil, nitrogen is released, stimulating the grass and causing the deeper green within the circle. Eventually the mushrooms parasitize the grass roots, especially those of bluegrass, red fescue, and bentgrass, causing them to die.

Fairy rings show up first as deep green circles of grass. Later, mushrooms appear along the edge.

The only sure way to eradicate the mushroom is to dig out the turf and soil to a depth of 2 feet, extending outward at least 1 foot beyond the edge of the circle. It's also possible to slow the fungus by drenching the soil with water to a depth of 2 feet. Some turf experts recommend fertilizing the rest of the lawn heavily to mask the green color of the ring. This practice, however, may encourage other diseases. You may be best off learning to live with the disease.

HITTING THE SLIME TRAIL

Slime molds (*Physarum cinereum* and *Mucilago spongiosa*) are rarely a serious problem. Even though the molds are fairly common worldwide, the causal fungi are not parasites, and do not harm the grass. But they do cover and disfigure it. Slime mold spore masses coat the grass, and look like cigarette ash on the surface of the blades. The spores can be easily wiped off. The overall infected area is usually of irregular shape, a few inches to several feet across. The mold may disappear after a couple of weeks, then reappear in the same place at the same time the following year. Mold typically appears in cool, humid fall weather.

Control is easy. No chemicals are required. Instead, simply remove the mold spores from the grass by rinsing with water during dry weather, or mowing and raking at any time.

DISEASE CLUES

To diagnose a disease or get help in doing so, you'll have to be able to answer the following questions.

- What species of grass is affected?
- When did the problem first appear?
- What were the daytime and nighttime temperatures when it appeared?
- Has the weather been exceptionally wet or dry?
- What were the first symptoms?
- How have the symptoms changed?
- Has the affected area grown larger, or changed shape?
- Do the grass leaves in the affected area show lesions, stripes, or patterns?
- Have pesticides or fertilizers been applied recently?
- Was the lawn watered recently? When and for how long?
- Is the area in sun or shade?
- Are there trees or shrubs growing near the area?
- Has anything been spilled in the area?

Then look for the disease under the conditions or situations that apply from the lists on the next two pages.

DISEASE SUSCEPTIBILITY

Susceptible Grass Species

All: Brown patch, drechslera, fairy ring, rusts, slime mold

Annual Ryegrass: Crown rust, dollar spot, fusarium patch, pythium

Bentgrass: Dollar spot, fusarium blight, fusarium patch, necrotic ring spot, ophiobolus, pythium, red thread, smuts, typhula

Bermudagrass: Dollar spot, drechslera, necrotic ring spot, powdery mildew, pythium, red thread, smuts

Bluegrass: Dollar spot, drechslera, fusarium blight, fusarium patch, leaf rust, necrotic ring spot, ophiobolus, powdery mildew, pythium, red thread, smuts, summer patch, typhula

Perennial Ryegrass: Crown rust, fusarium patch, ophiobolus, red thread, smuts, typhula

Red Fescue: Dollar spot, drechslera, fusarium blight, fusarium patch, necrotic ring spot, ophiobolus, powdery mildew, pythium, red thread

Tall Fescue: Crown rust, fusarium patch, ophiobolus, pythium, typhula

Zoysia: Dollar spot, leaf rust

Diseases by Region (U.S.)

All: Brown patch, dollar spot, drechslera fusarium blight, rusts, slime molds

Midwest: Brown patch, dollar spot, fusarium, leaf spot, melting out, snow mold

North Central: Fusarium patch, leaf spot, melting out, pythium

Northeast: Brown patch, dollar spot, fusarium blight, melting out, red thread, snow mold

Northwest: Ophiobolus, red thread

Southeast: Brown patch, dollar spot, drechslera, fusarium, leaf spot, red thread, rusts, snow mold

Southwest: Brown patch, leaf spot

Diseases by Season

Spring: Necrotic ring spot, pink patch, red thread, typhula

Early Summer: Brown patch, fusarium blight, stripe smut

Late Summer: Brown patch, dollar spot, powdery mildew, pythium, rusts, stripe smut

Fall: Fusarium patch, necrotic ring spot, pink patch, red thread

Preferred Conditions for Disease

Cool Weather (below 60°F): Drechslera, fusarium patch, ophiobolus, powdery mildew, red thread, slime mold, smuts, thyphia

Warm Weather (60° to 80°F): Dollar spot, necrotic ring spot, red thread

Hot Weather (above 80°F): Brown patch, fusarium blight, pythium, rusts

Dry Weather: Dollar spot, drechslera, melting out, red thread, rusts

Wet Weather: Brown patch (hot and humid), fairy ring, leaf spot, melting out (cool), ophiobolis, pythium, red thread, slime mold, stripe smut, thyphia (cool to cold)

(continued)

DISEASE SUSCEPTIBILITY—Continued

Preferred Conditions for Disease—Continued

High Nitrogen Levels: Brown patch, drechslera, fusarium blight, fusarium patch, powdery mildew, pythium

Low Nitrogen Levels: Brown patch, dollar spot, melting out, red thread, rusts

Low pH: Dollar spot, stripe smut

Shade: Powdery mildew, pythium

Low Mowing: Drechslera, fusarium blight, necrotic ring spot

Thatch: Fusarium blight, fusarium patch, leaf spot, slime mold, stripe smut, typhula

Disease Pattern Shapes

Circle: Brown patch, snow mold, typhula

Irregular: Pythium, slime mold

Patch: Ophiobolus, red thread

Ring: Fairy ring

Spot: Dollar spot, fusarium blight, necrotic ring spot, stripe smut

Unpatterned: Drechslera, powdery mildew, rusts

Disease Color

Green: Fairy ring

Pale Green: Fusarium blight, smuts

Pink: Red thread

Red: Drechslera

Red to Tan: Fusarium blight, rusts

Tan: Brown patch, dollar spot, drechslera, fusarium patch, ophiobolus

White: Powdery mildew, typhula

White (and Black): Slime mold

Yellow: Fusarium patch

BIBLIOGRAPHY

Ball, Jeff, narrator. *How to Care for Your Lawn.* Indianapolis, Ind.: Kartes Video Communications, 1986. A Yardening © VHS videocassette.

Bennett, Jennifer, ed. *The Harrowsmith Landscaping Book.* Camden East, Ontario: Camden House Publishing Ltd., 1985.

————. *Ground Covers: A Harrowsmith Gardener's Guide.* Camden East, Ontario: Camden House Publishing Ltd., 1987.

Better Homes and Gardens. *Your Yard.* Des Moines, Iowa: Meredith Corporation, 1984.

Commonsense Pest Control Quarterly. Berkeley: Bio Integral Resource Center.

Editors of *Reader's Digest. Reader's Digest Practical Guide to Home Landscaping.* Pleasantville, N. Y.: The Reader's Digest Association, 1972.

Hall, Walter. *Barnacle Parp's Guide to Garden and Yard Power Tools.* Emmaus, Pa.: Rodale Press, 1983.

Leighton, Phebe, and Calvin Simonds. *The New American Landscape Gardener.* Emmaus, Pa.: Rodale Press, 1987.

MacCaskey, Michael. *Lawns and Ground Covers: How to Select, Grow and Enjoy.* Tucson, Ariz.: HP Books, 1982.

Smith, Michael D., ed. *The Ortho Problem Solver,* 2nd ed. San Francisco: Ortho Information Services, 1984.

Smith, Miranda, and Anna Carr. *Rodale's Garden Insect, Disease, and Weed Identification Guide.* Emmaus, Pa.: Rodale Press, 1988.

Wirth, Thomas. *The Victory Garden Landscape Guide.* Boston: Little, Brown and Co., 1984.

INDEX

Page references in italics indicate illustrations and photos. Page references in boldface indicate tables.